Your surname

Colour your shirt in

Shirt number

This book belongs to ....

Age ....

My favourite team is ....

My favourite player is ....

My highlight of 2025 was ....

....

CW01456588

WELCOME!

IT'S BEEN ANOTHER DRAMATIC YEAR of footy — packed full of titles, trophies and breakout talent. We've seen teams make history and players made into stars. Join us as we look baaa-ck on the greatest games and goated moments of 2025!

WHAT'S INSIDE YOUR 2026 ANNUAL?

THE BIG WINNERS OF 2025

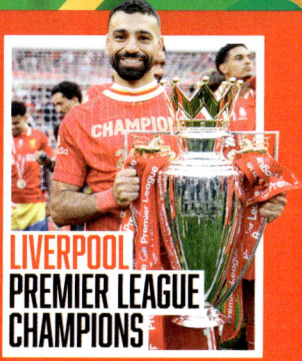

LIVERPOOL
PREMIER LEAGUE CHAMPIONS

ARNE SLOT, in his first season at Anfield, led the Reds to their 20th league title — equalling Man. United's record for title wins!

PSG
UCL WINNERS

PSG BECAME everyone's second fave team. They smashed Inter Milan 5-0 to lift the Champions League — a record UCL final win!

CHELSEA
WSL WINNERS

CHELSEA GOT a new manager, but that didn't stop them winning. It was their sixth WSL title in a row!

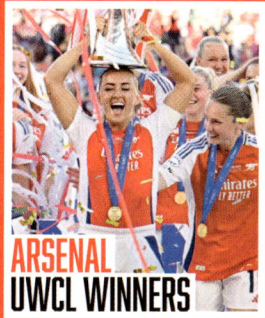

ARSENAL
UWCL WINNERS

THE GUNNERS beat Barcelona 1-0 to become the first English team to win the Women's Champions League since way back in 2007!

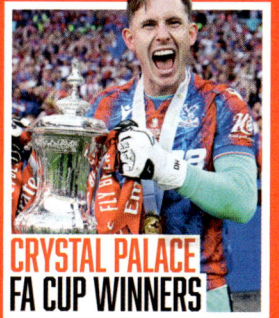

CRYSTAL PALACE
FA CUP WINNERS

THE EAGLES stunned the world when they beat favourites Man. City at Wembley 1-0 to claim their first EVER trophy!

---

96 PAGES OF BALLER BRILLIANCE!

2026 LEVEL UP!

AMATEUR
PROFESSIONAL
WORLD CLASS

P38 18 EPIC CHALLENGES FOR 2026!

DREAM TEAMS
PAST, PRESENT AND FUTURE!

P62 DREAM TEAMS!

GOAL HERO POSTERS!

We're biggin' up the best scorers in the game with **11 beautiful posters!**

5

THE LOL! ZONE!

With Adam la Llama!

What's this again? A trombone?

100% DEFINITELY, COMPLETELY TRUE FOOTY FACTS!

YEP, THESE ARE ALL TRUE FACTS, THERE'S NOTHING MADE UP HERE, NOPE!*

ALESSIA RUSSO'S PET CORGI IS 63FT TALL!

You do not wanna scoop that poop!

I actually can see him!

COLE PALMER NEVER LEAVES HOME WITHOUT A FRAMED PHOTO OF WWE STAR JOHN CENA!

GOAL KING!

★★ KYLIAN ★★

MBAPPE

FRANCE

90 CAPS / 50 GOALS

BBC

MATCH OF THE DAY MAGAZINE

MASCOT MISMATCH!

Tick the mascots you'd find in the Premier League – the others are just Prem pretenders!

1
A Grecian the Lion ☑
B Stamford the Lion ☑

2
A Ritter Keule ☑
B Robin Hood ☑

3
A Wolfie ☑
B Wolfi ☑

4
A Marinos-kun and Marinosuke ☑
B Gully ☑

5
A Gunnersaurus ☑
B Dino Hermann ☑

6
A Moonbeam ☑
B Steelman ☑

ANSWERS ON p92!

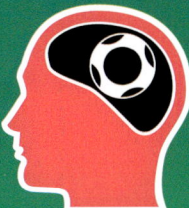

YOUR FOOTY BRAIN POWER

YOUR SCORE ☐ /6	
6	GENIUS
5	PROFESSIONAL
4	SEMI-PRO
3	AMATEUR
1-2	SUNDAY LEAGUE
0	OH NO, DISASTER

THE SALAH STORY!

IT HASN'T been an easy journey to the top for Mohamed Salah! The Egyptian King took the long route to the big time, working tirelessly to improve his game and overcome setbacks. It's all paid off! He's now a two-time Prem winner, a Champions League winner and has about 22 million other awards on his mantelpiece. Here's how the Liverpool star did it!

96 CAM

Zidane

PAC	SHO	PAS	DRI	DEF	PHY
86	92	96	96	76	86

96 ST

CM

Ronaldo

PAC	SHO	PAS	DRI	DEF	PHY
96	96	81	96	45	80

HIS BEGINNINGS!

SALAH FALLS in love with football aged eight, watching legends like Zinedine Zidane and Ronaldo ball out in the Champions League. He joins Egyptian team Al-Mokawloon at 14 — and has to travel four hours on buses just to get to training!

OFF TO EUROPE!

HIS FORM for club and country earns Salah a move to Swiss side Basel in 2012. The move isn't easy for him though — he's living alone and can't speak the language. But he works hard and soon scores some huge goals for his new team — including against Spurs!

CHELSEA CALLS!

SALAH ALSO scores three goals against Chelsea while at Basel. Those goals convince the Blues to sign him for £11m in January 2014. The switch doesn't work out for 21-year-old Mo though. He only plays 19 games before being shipped off!

SENT AWAY!

MO IS not wanted at Chelsea, but a loan move to Italian team Fiorentina is exactly what he needs. Salah crushes it for the Viola, helping them get to the semi-finals of the Europa League. Lots of other clubs are soon interested in signing him!

SERIE A STAR!

SALAH DECIDES on another Italian adventure for the 2015-16 season, heading to the capital Rome on loan. Salah's epic form continues — he finishes as the team's top scorer and wins the club's Player of the Season award!

SALAH'S STORY...

ROMA SUCCESS!

THE ROMANS love him so much, they turn his loan into a permanent deal for £12m. He hits 19 goals in 41 games in the Italian capital. But after just one season he is a man in demand — and Roma can't keep hold of him!

FINALLY RED!

SALAH JOINS Liverpool in June 2017 for a club record £36.9m. The Reds had actually tried to sign him when he joined Chelsea. The forward is buzzing to finally join Liverpool, partly because he used to play as them on FIFA!

GOOD AND BAD!

SALAH SMASHES it in his first season, winning PFA Player of the Year and the Prem Golden Boot. The season ends in heartbreak though. A tangle with Real Madrid defender Sergio Ramos in the 2018 Champions League final injures his shoulder. He has to go off and Liverpool lose 3-1!

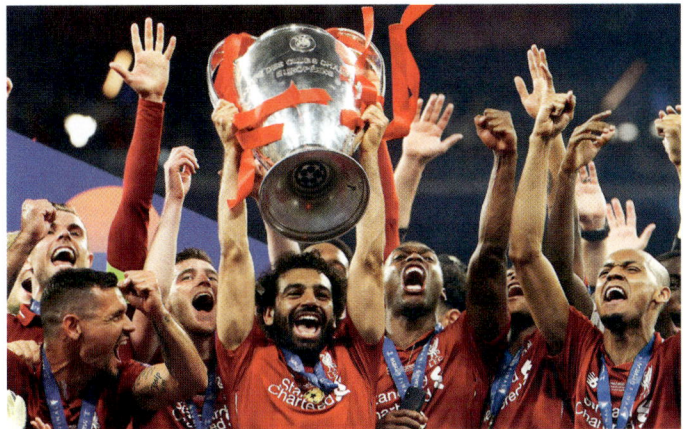

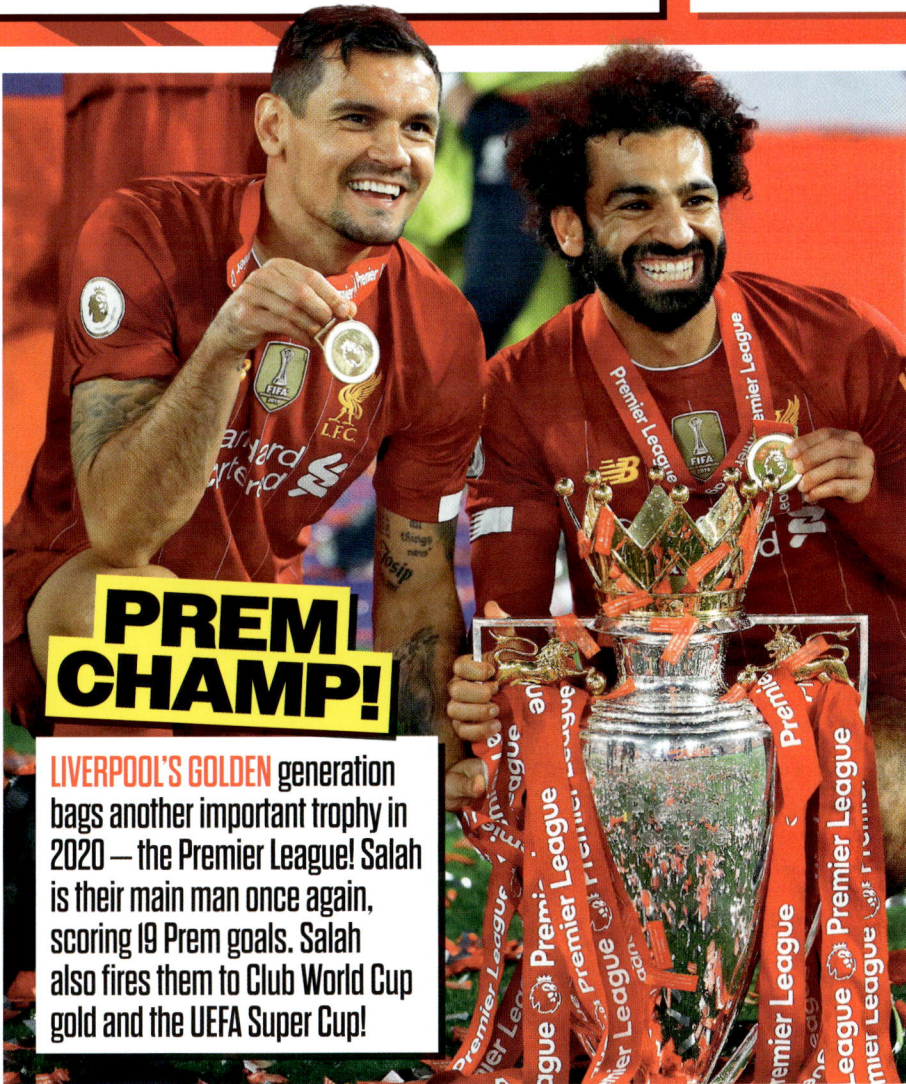

UCL REDEMPTION!

ONE YEAR after getting injured in the UCL final, Mo leads Liverpool's dream team to European glory! Salah scores the opener in the 2019 UCL final to help Liverpool beat Tottenham 2-0. He's the first Egyptian to ever win the Champions League!

PREM CHAMP!

LIVERPOOL'S GOLDEN generation bags another important trophy in 2020 — the Premier League! Salah is their main man once again, scoring 19 Prem goals. Salah also fires them to Club World Cup gold and the UEFA Super Cup!

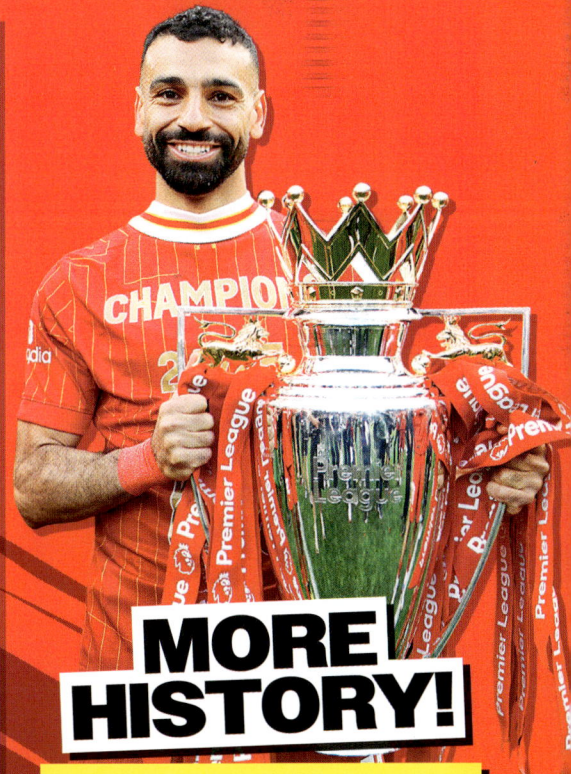

MORE HISTORY!

SALAH HAS continued to be incredible ever since, breaking records season after season. He bagged another Prem trophy in 2025 and signed a new contract to keep the good times rolling on Merseyside. All that hard work definitely paid off!

SALAH'S STORY...

FACT FILE

FULL NAME Mohamed Salah Hamed Mahrous Ghaly
DATE OF BIRTH 15 June 1992 (age 33)
PLACE OF BIRTH Nagrig, Egypt
HEIGHT 5ft 9in
POSITION Right-winger
STRONG FOOT Left

THROUGH THE YEARS!

Check out Mo's most iconic FIFA shields from over the years!

FIFA 14

FIFA 17

FIFA 22

FC 24

FC 25

SALAH'S SUPER CAREER!

AND WHAT A CAREER HE'S HAD!

TROPHY TIME!

These are all the trophies Mo has won so far!

HIS CAREER IN NUMBERS!

2 x SWISS SUPER LEAGUE

1 x COMMUNITY SHIELD

3 x LEAGUE CUP

1 x FA CUP

1 x UEFA SUPER CUP

2 x PREMIER LEAGUE

1 x CHAMPIONS LEAGUE

1 x CLUB WORLD CUP

AL-MOKAWLOON 2006-12

GAMES	45
GOALS	12
ASSISTS	6

BASEL 2012-14

GAMES	79
GOALS	20
ASSISTS	14

CHELSEA 2014-16

GAMES	19
GOALS	2
ASSISTS	3

FIORENTINA 2015

GAMES	26
GOALS	9
ASSISTS	4

ROMA 2015-17

GAMES	83
GOALS	34
ASSISTS	21

LIVERPOOL 2017-NOW

GAMES	401
GOALS	245
ASSISTS	113

Stats correct up to 30 July 2025.

17

A YEAR IN FOOTBALL!

I POINT for each correct answer!

2025 was a bumper year of footy – but were you paying attention? Here's your chance to prove it!

1
Who won Premier League Player of the Year?
- A Mohamed Salah ☐
- B Erling Haaland ☐
- C Declan Rice ☐

2
This new trophy was unveiled – but which competition was it for?
- A French Cup ☐
- B Club World Cup ☐
- C MLS Cup ☐

3
This guy became the new England boss. Name him!
- A Jonas Eidevall ☐
- B Steve Cooper ☐
- C Thomas Tuchel ☐

4
The Lionesses played which home nation at Euro 2025?
- A Scotland ☐
- B Wales ☐
- C Northern Ireland ☐

5
This ledge was everywhere – but what's her name?
- A Maddli ☐
- B Bekki ☐
- C Kelli ☐

6
Which massive Midlands club won League One?
- A Aston Villa ☐
- B Birmingham ☐
- C Walsall ☐

7
Which defender scored a header in the 2025 EFL Cup final?
- A Cristian Romero ☐
- B Virgil van Dijk ☐
- C Dan Burn ☐

8
England ace Keira Walsh joined Chelsea from which club?
- A Barcelona ☐
- B Juventus ☐
- C PSG ☐

9
Which keeper admitted he wears the same pants for every game?
- A Jordan Pickford ☐
- B Ederson ☐
- C Gianluigi Donnarumma ☐

ANSWERS ON p92!

YOUR FOOTY BRAIN POWER

- 9 GENIUS
- 7 PROFESSIONAL
- 5 SEMI-PRO
- 3 AMATEUR
- 1 SUNDAY LEAGUE
- 0 OH NO, DISASTER

YOUR SCORE ☐/9

GOAL KING!

193
CAPS

112
GOALS

LIONEL

MESSI

ARGENTINA

BBC MATCH OF THE DAY MAGAZINE

THE 20

BIGGEST FOOTBALL CLUBS IN THE WORLD!

WE CRUNCHED the numbers, totted up the trophies and checked out the history to reveal who really is the biggest club on the planet!

THE RATINGS!

Each club is rated out of 20 in these five categories:

LEGACY
How big is their impact on football history?

GLOBAL FAME
How famous are they around the world?

TROPHIES
Have they won loads at home and abroad?

FAN PASSION
How noisy and colourful are their supporters?

STAR POWER
How many iconic players have worn the shirt?

20 BORUSSIA DORTMUND

GERMANY

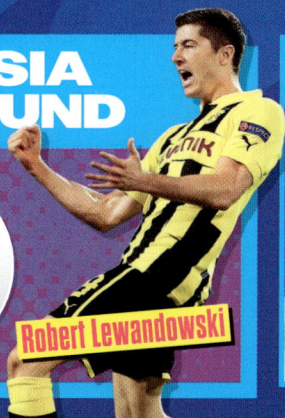
Robert Lewandowski

19 CELTIC

SCOTLAND

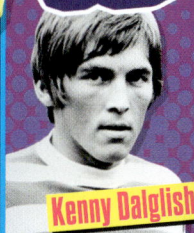
Kenny Dalglish

18 FLAMENGO

Romario

BRAZIL

17 NAPOLI

ITALY

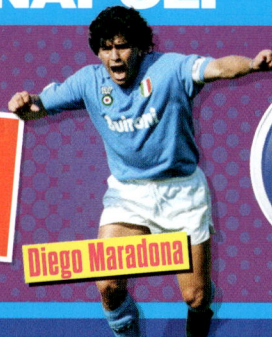
Diego Maradona

16 BENFICA

PORTUGAL

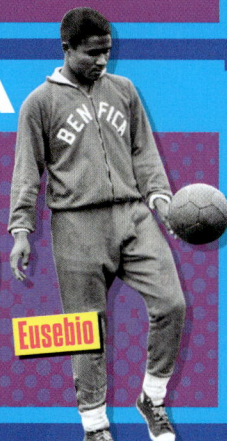
Eusebio

15 RIVER PLATE

Enzo Francescoli

ARGENTINA

14 BOCA JUNIORS

ARGENTINA

Carlos Tevez

13 PSG

FRANCE

Kylian Mbappe

12 MAN. CITY

Erling Haaland

ENGLAND

11 CHELSEA

ENGLAND

Didier Drogba

10 AJAX

NETHERLANDS

THE BIO

THE TOTAL Football Factory! Ajax introduced the world to a tekkier game and produced world-class talent – think Johan Cruyff, Marco van Basten, Dennis Bergkamp and Frenkie de Jong!

THE ICON
Johan Cruyff

THE CLUB FACTS

FOUNDED 1900
NICKNAME Godenzonen (Sons of the Gods)
STADIUM Johan Cruyff Arena (55,865)
RECORD SIGNING Steven Bergwijn (£26m, 2022)

THE TROPHY CABINET

League titles	36
UCL/European Cups	4
Domestic cups	20

THE CURRENT STAR
Kenneth Taylor

📚 16 / 20	🔥 12 / 20
🌍 9 / 20	🤩 16 / 20
🏆 15 / 20	TOTAL 68 / 100

9 ARSENAL

ENGLAND

THE BIO

FROM THE Invincible season, in 2003-04, to homegrown heroes, the London club is a fusion of flair, footy traditions – and the holder of a record 14 FA Cups!

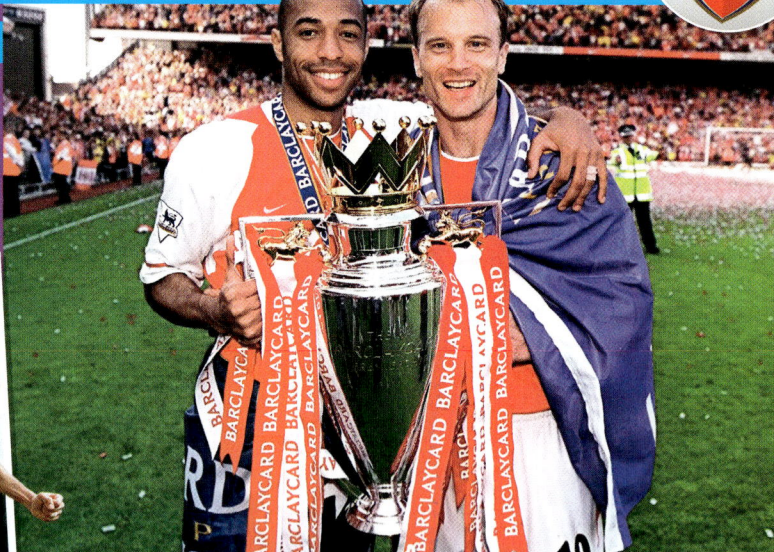

THE ICON
Thierry Henry

THE CLUB FACTS

FOUNDED 1886
NICKNAME The Gunners
STADIUM The Emirates (60,704)
RECORD SIGNING Declan Rice (£105m, 2023)

THE TROPHY CABINET

League titles	13
UCL/European Cups	0
Domestic cups	16

THE CURRENT STAR
Bukayo Saka

📚 15 / 20	🔥 11 / 20
🌍 15 / 20	🤩 14 / 20
🏆 14 / 20	TOTAL 69 / 100

8 INTER MILAN

ITALY

THE BIO

FOUNDED ON fierce rivalries, fire comebacks and a ferocious will to win, Inter are Italy's most-feared team. In 2010, they became the first Italian club to win the treble!

THE CLUB FACTS

FOUNDED 1908
NICKNAME I Nerazzurri (The Black and Blues)
STADIUM San Siro (75,817)
RECORD SIGNING
Romelu Lukaku (£68.2m, 2019)

THE TROPHY CABINET

League titles		20
UCL/European Cups		3
Domestic cups		9

THE ICON
Ronaldo

📖 15 / 20	🔥 16 / 20	
🌍 15 / 20	😆 18 / 20	
🏆 15 / 20	TOTAL 79 / 100	

THE CURRENT STAR
Lautaro Martinez

7 JUVENTUS

ITALY

THE BIO

ICONIC CLUB, iconic players and that iconic kit! Juventus is Serie A's most successful club — between 2011 and 2020 they won nine league titles in a row!

THE CLUB FACTS

FOUNDED 1897
NICKNAME The Old Lady
STADIUM Juventus Stadium (41,507)
RECORD SIGNING
Cristiano Ronaldo (£100m, 2018)

THE TROPHY CABINET

League titles		36
UCL/European Cups		2
Domestic cups		15

THE ICON
Alessandro Del Piero

📚 16 / 20	🔥 14 / 20	
🌍 16 / 20	😆 18 / 20	
🏆 16 / 20	TOTAL 80 / 100	

THE CURRENT STAR
Kenan Yildiz

6 AC MILAN

ITALY

THE BIO

MILAN STYLE, defensive dynasties and pure European class — only Real Madrid have more European Cups than the Rossoneri!

OPEL

THE ICON
Paolo Maldini

THE CLUB FACTS

FOUNDED 1899
NICKNAME Rossoneri (The Red and Blacks)
STADIUM San Siro (75,817)
RECORD SIGNING Rafeal Leao (£42.2m, 2019)

THE TROPHY CABINET

League titles	19
UCL/European Cups	7
Domestic cups	5

THE CURRENT STAR
Rafeal Leao

📚	18 / 20	🔥	16 / 20
🌍	16 / 20	🤩	17 / 20
🏆	18 / 20	**TOTAL 85 / 100**	

5 LIVERPOOL

ENGLAND

THE BIO

THE REDS dominated football in the 1970s and 1980s, and now they're back bossing it again. Their historic home stadium Anfield has one of the best atmospheres around!

Carlsberg

THE ICON
Steven Gerrard

THE CLUB FACTS

FOUNDED 1892
NICKNAME The Reds
STADIUM Anfield (61,276)
RECORD SIGNING Florian Wirtz (£116m, 2025)

THE TROPHY CABINET

League titles	20
UCL/European Cups	6
Domestic cups	18

THE CURRENT STAR
Mohamed Salah

📚	18 / 20	🔥	19 / 20
🌍	15 / 20	🤩	15 / 20
🏆	18 / 20	**TOTAL 85 / 100**	

4 BAYERN MUNICH

GERMANY

THE BIO

THESE GERMAN giants are known for silverware and their singing supporters. Plus, Bayern have an awesome academy that has gifted football some of the all-time greats!

THE CLUB FACTS

FOUNDED 1900
NICKNAME Die Bayern
STADIUM Allianz Arena (75,024)
RECORD SIGNING Harry Kane (£82m, 2023)

THE TROPHY CABINET

League titles 🟡		34
UCL/European Cups 🏆		6
Domestic cups 🏆		20

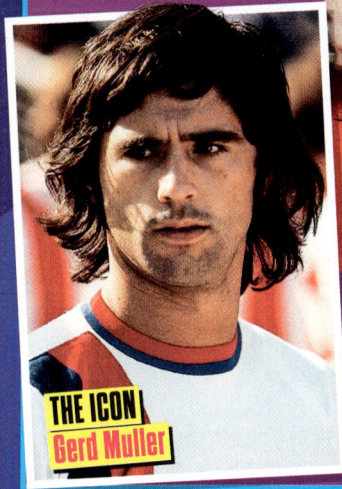

THE ICON
Gerd Muller

📚	18 / 20	🔥	20 / 20
🌍	15 / 20	🤩	17 / 20
🏆	19 / 20	**TOTAL 89 / 100**	

THE CURRENT STAR
Harry Kane

3 MAN. UNITED

ENGLAND

THE BIO

MAN. UNITED are famous for winning with teams full of academy graduates — first, the Busby Babes in the 1950s, and then in the 1990s, under ledge manager Sir Alex Ferguson!

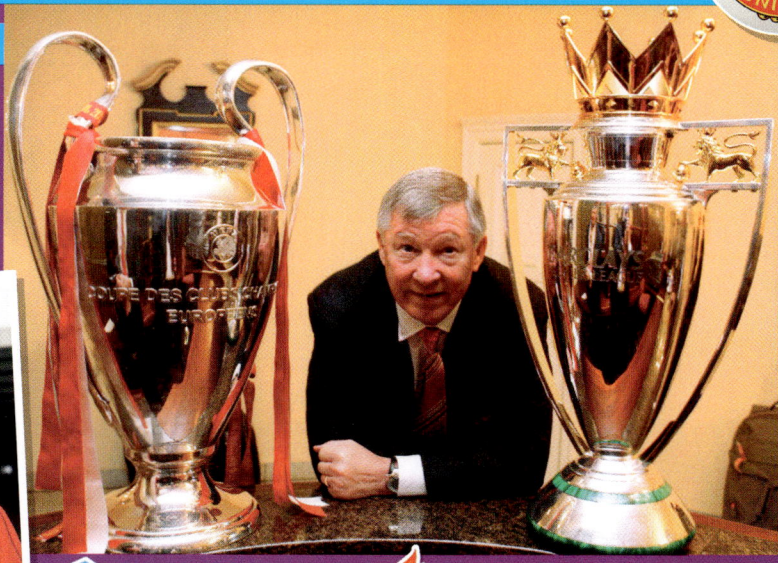

THE CLUB FACTS

FOUNDED 1878
NICKNAME The Red Devils
STADIUM Old Trafford (74,197)
RECORD SIGNING Paul Pogba (£89m, 2016)

THE TROPHY CABINET

League titles 👑		20
UCL/European Cups 🏆		3
Domestic cups 🏆		19

THE ICON
Bobby Charlton

📚	20 / 20	🔥	15 / 20
🌍	20 / 20	🤩	18 / 20
🏆	17 / 20	**TOTAL 90 / 100**	

THE CURRENT STAR
Bruno Fernandes

2 BARCELONA

SPAIN

THE BIO

BARCA'S ACADEMY is the best in the world. They've produced tons of tiki-taka tekky talents like Andres Iniesta, Xavi and of course the all-time GOAT, Lionel Messi!

THE CLUB FACTS

FOUNDED 1899
NICKNAME Blaugrana
STADIUM Nou Camp (99,354)
RECORD SIGNING
Philippe Coutinho (£142m, 2018)

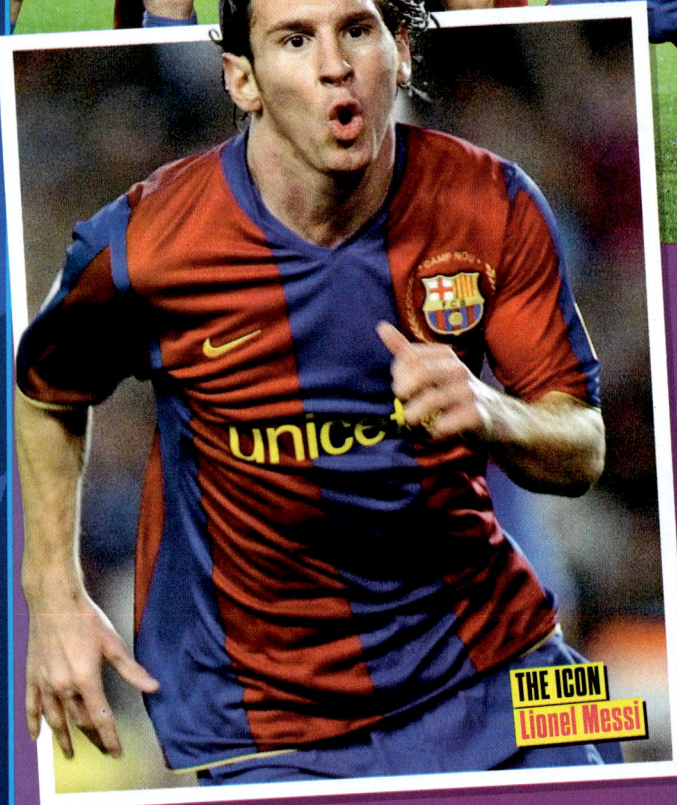

THE ICON
Lionel Messi

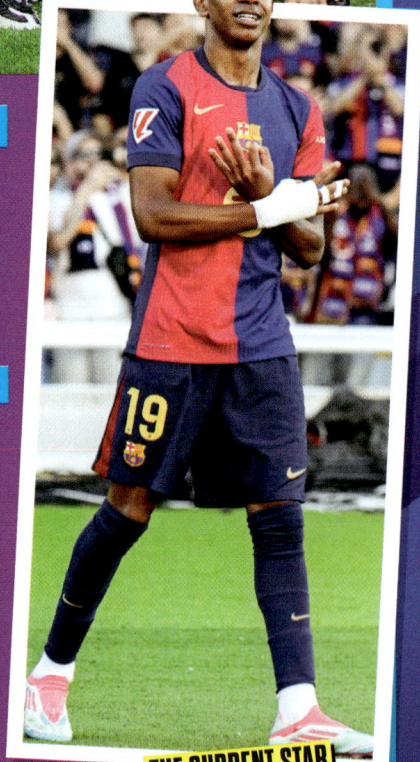

THE CURRENT STAR
Lamine Yamal

THE TROPHY CABINET

League titles	28
UCL/European Cups	5
Domestic cups	32

📚	20 / 20	🔥	18 / 20
🌎	19 / 20	🤩	20 / 20
🏆	19 / 20	**TOTAL**	**96 / 100**

1 REAL MADRID

SPAIN

THE BIO

REAL MADRID may splash the cash on Galactico signings, but they back it up on the pitch — the Spanish giants have won twice as many Champions League trophies as the next best!

THE CLUB FACTS

FOUNDED 1902
NICKNAME Los Blancos
STADIUM Santiago Bernabeu (78,297)
RECORD SIGNING Eden Hazard (£149m, 2019)

THE ICON
Cristiano Ronaldo

THE CURRENT STAR
Jude Bellingham

THE TROPHY CABINET

League titles	36
UCL/European Cups	15
Domestic cups	20

📚	19 / 20	🔥	18 / 20
🌍	20 / 20	🤩	20 / 20
🏆	20 / 20	**TOTAL**	**97 / 100**

27

THE LOL! ZONE!

MEME-WHILE...

INTERNATIONAL FOOTY CAN BE WELL SILLY!

Everything else is in the wash!

WHEN YOUR MATE TAKES OWN-CLOTHES DAY TOO FAR!

The driver's so going to eat my Babybel!

WHEN YOU LEAVE YOUR LUNCH ON THE COACH!

Eyyyy, you glazed dozen legend!

WHEN YOUR MATE TURNS UP WITH DOUGHNUTS!

Quick selfie, then more Mario...

WHEN YOUR MUM ASKS IF YOU GOT TO YOUR MATE'S HOUSE OK!

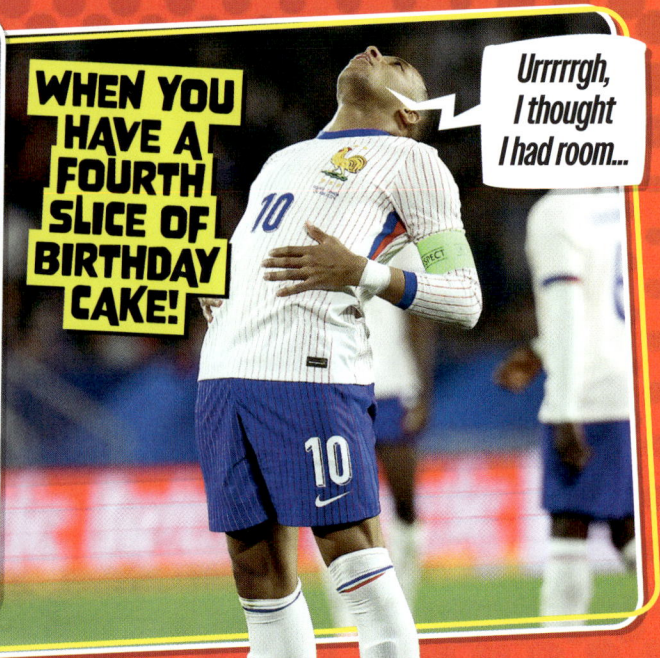

WHEN YOU HAVE A FOURTH SLICE OF BIRTHDAY CAKE!

Urrrrrgh, I thought I had room...

GOAL KING!

CRISTIANO

RONALDO

PORTUGAL

221 CAPS

138 GOALS

BBC MATCH OF THE DAY MAGAZINE

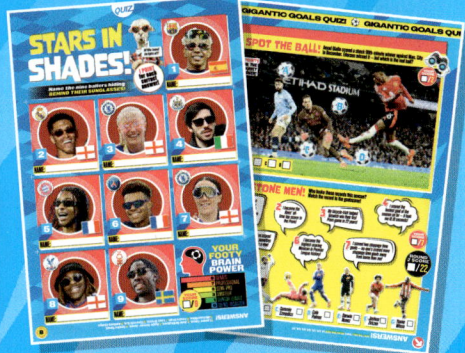

No.1 FOR WOMEN'S FOOTY!

No.1 FOR LOLS!

No.1 FOR QUIZZES!

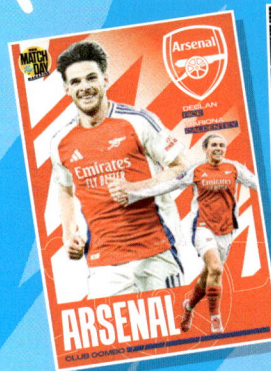

No.1 FOR SKILLS ADVICE!

No.1 FOR POSTERS!

THE BIGGEST STARS LOVE MATCH OF THE DAY MAGAZINE!

PRIDE OF ENGL

It's time to rewind to Euro 2025 — and what a rollercoaster ride it was. We look back at the Lionesses' twisting, turning and title-winning tournament!

THE GROUP GAMES

KICKSTART KEIRA!

THE LIONESS Keira Walsh

THE GAME France 2-1 England **THE DATE** 5 July

The tourney gets off to a tough start. England get bossed — and beaten — by Les Bleues. Keira Walsh kickstarts the comeback with a goal in the 87th minute — but it's too late for the Lionesses!

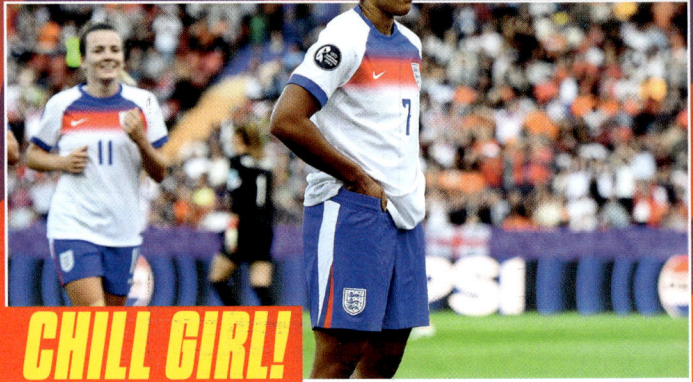

CHILL GIRL!

THE LIONESS Lauren James

THE GAME England 4-0 Netherlands **THE DATE** 9 July

The Lionesses can't afford to lose — and the pressure is on. Except Lauren James doesn't know pressure. She bags a worldie and pulls out the 'chill girl' cele. COLD!

PROPER ENGLAND!

THE LIONESS Georgia Stanway

THE GAME England 4-0 Netherlands **THE DATE** 9 July

Georgia Stanway promises a 'Proper England' performance — and the fans get one! She springs high after scoring just before half-time. The Dutch are demolished — and England are on their way!

DRAGONS SLAYED!

THE LIONESS Ella Toone

THE GAME England 6-1 Wales **THE DATE** 13 July

Wales bring thousands of fans, but the Lionesses bring the fire. Tooney is on top form; England's No.10 scores and assists for bestie Alessia Russo. The win means The Lionesses are through!

AND!

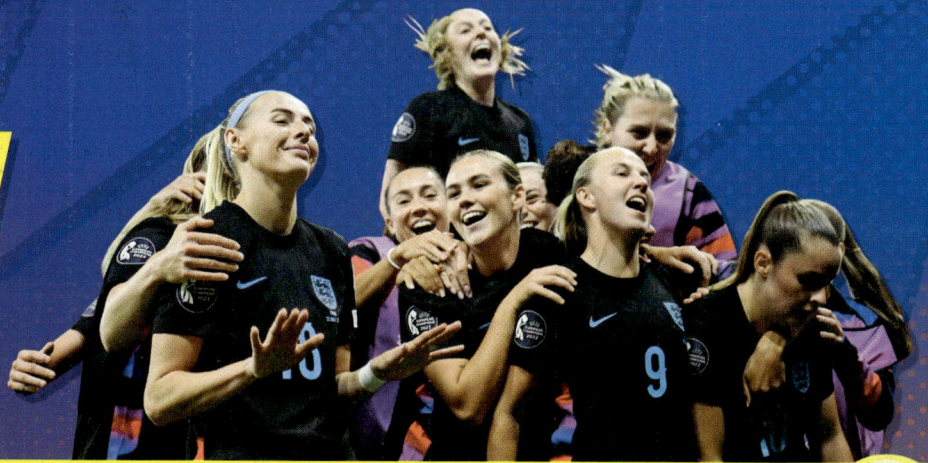

😃 THE QUARTER-FINAL 🎧

THE COMEBACK QUEENS!

THE LIONESSES Chloe Kelly & Michelle Agyemang

THE GAME Sweden 2-2 England **THE DATE** 17 July

2-0 down after 25 minutes — the Lionesses are going out. They need a hero — and they have two. Super subs Chloe Kelly and Michelle Agyemang rescue England. The game goes to penalties!

EURO STARS!

It was Lucy Bronze's seventh major tourney for the Lionesses — she even played it with a broken leg!

NO-SE PROBLEM!

THE LIONESS Hannah Hampton

THE GAME Sweden 2-2 England **THE DATE** 17 July

Who needs two nostrils? Not Hannah Hampton! After getting a clattering — and a nosebleed — the England keeper calmly carries on and pulls off two huge penalty saves. What a warrior!

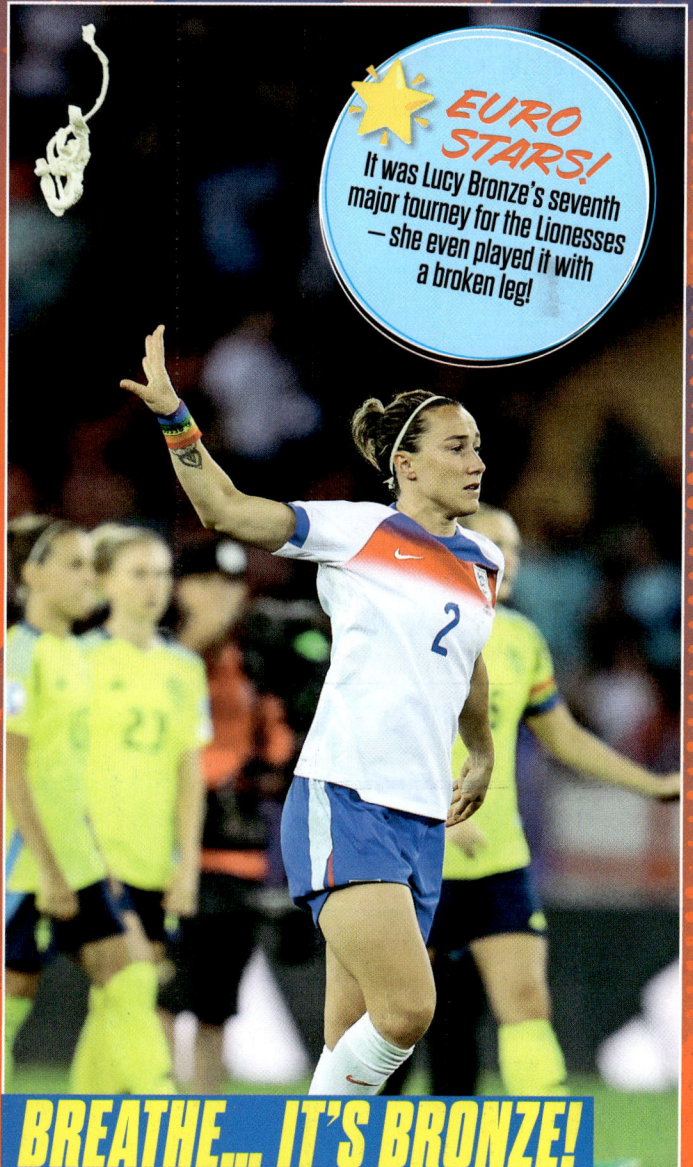

BREATHE... IT'S BRONZE!

THE LIONESS Lucy Bronze

THE GAME Sweden 2-2 England **THE DATE** 17 July

Will anyone score their penalty? Step forward Lucy Bronze. The Chelsea star rips off her strapping and smashes the ball into the net. The comeback is complete — England are in the semis!

THE SEMI-FINAL

EURO STARS!

Agyemang became the first teenager to score twice at a Euros since 2009.

SWEET AGYEMANG!

THE LIONESS Michelle Agyemang

THE GAME England 2-1 Italy **THE DATE** 22 July

Another late — and great — escape! It's the 96th minute and England are going out. But they never, ever give up. Super sub Michelle Agyemang slams it home with seconds to spare. 1-1!

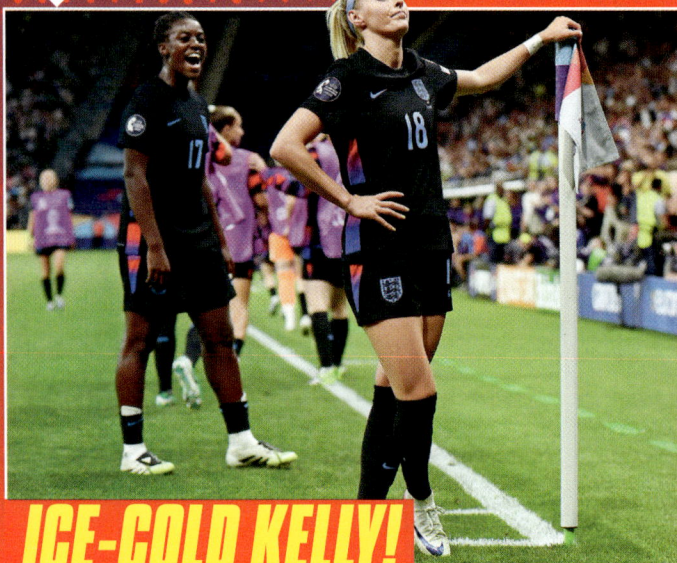

ICE-COLD KELLY!

THE LIONESS Chloe Kelly

THE GAME England 2-1 Italy **THE DATE** 22 July

Extra time, extra drama! England throw everything at Italy — until Beth Mead is hauled to the floor. Penalty! Chloe Kelly's 119th-minute pen is saved, but she nets the rebound. England are in the final!

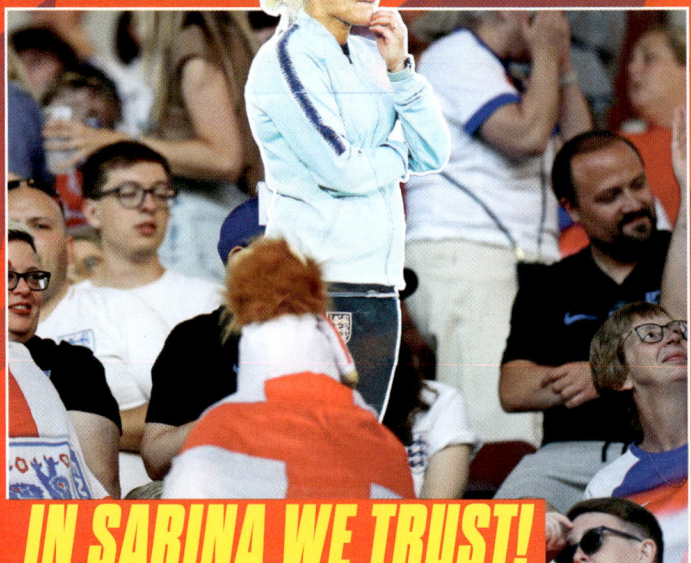

IN SARINA WE TRUST!

THE COACH Sarina Wiegman

THE GAME England 2-1 Italy **THE DATE** 22 July

Take a bow, Sarina! The supercoach steers England into their third straight major tourney final — and her fifth in a row. No other coach in the history of football has completed that!

THE FINAL

HEADER HERO!

THE LIONESS Alessia Russo

THE GAME England 1-1 Spain **THE DATE** 27 July

Spain are in control. England can feel their crown slipping away. They need a spark — it comes, again, from supersub Chloe Kelly. She crosses to Alessia Russo who heads home. England are level!

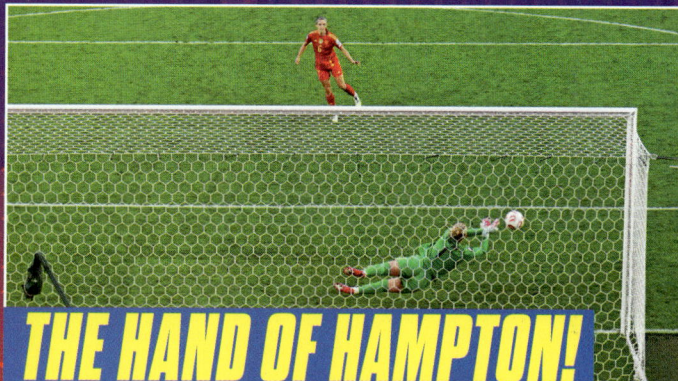

THE HAND OF HAMPTON!

THE LIONESS Hannah Hampton

THE GAME England 1-1 Spain **THE DATE** 27 July

It's 1-1 after extra-time and that only means one thing... penalties! Hannah faces Ballon d'Or winner Aitana Bonmati. The shot-stopper pulls off a spectacular save. Advantage England!

QUEEN CHLOE!

HOP, STEP... and a thump! Chloe Kelly converts her trademark pen. She scores the winning goal in a Euro final — for the second time!

WINNERS
UEFA WOMEN'S EURO 2025

EURO STARS! A record 11 different players scored for England at the Euros. Teamwork!

THE HISTORY MAKERS!

THEY DID IT! The Lionesses are European champions again — and the first team to win back-to-back titles since 2013. We'll leave the final word to England's penalty queen Chloe Kelly, who said: "The first time felt so nice, we had to do it twice!"

BBC MATCH OF THE DAY magazine

SCORE BIG WITH THE **PERFECT GIFT!**

SUBSCRIBE BY 31 AUGUST 2026

THE UK'S **BEST-SELLING** FOOTY MAGAZINE!

PAY **£42.99** *for 12 issues, saving 32%!**

SUBSCRIBE TODAY

VISIT buysubscriptions.com/**MDPSANN25**

GOAL KING!

ERLING HAALAND

NORWAY

**43 CAPS
42 GOALS**

2026

LEVEL UP!

WE'VE SET the challenges, now it's time to take your footy fandom to new heights!

1

SCORE FIVE PENS IN A ROW!

THIS MIGHT SOUND tough but pick a rubbish keeper, and keep taking them until you hit the magic five in a row!

COMPLETED IT! ✓

2

DESIGN A MASCOT!

DRAW A NEW mascot for your fave team. Check out these weird mascots from outside of football for some inspo!

COMPLETED IT! ✓

3

WATCH SOME FOOTY ON TV!

HEAD ON OVER to the Sport section of BBC iPlayer and who knows what you'll find. Maybe you'll learn how to win the UCL or find out all about Kylian Mbappe!

COMPLETED IT! ✓

4

WIN A TROPHY!

IT'S GAMING TIME! Hop onto your fave footy game and bag yourself some silverware. It might be the only time your team wins any!

COMPLETED IT! ✓

PROFESSIONAL!

5

LEARN A WORLD CUP FACT!

FIND OUT SOMETHING cool about the World Cup, then see if your friends and family already knew it. We've got a fact for you here if you want it...

DID YOU KNOW?
Some people think the USA are rubbish at footy — but they won bronze at the 1930 World Cup!

COMPLETED IT! ✓

6

SCORE A TOP BINS BANGER!

CHANNEL YOUR INNER Declan Rice and fire a free-kick into the absolute top corner. You don't have to do it against Real Madrid though!

COMPLETED IT! ✓

TEAM YOUR TOYS!

GRAB YOUR TOYS and create the best five-a-side team you can. You can do this with your fave TV or gaming characters too. We're putting Robin on the wing!

7

COMPLETED IT! ✓

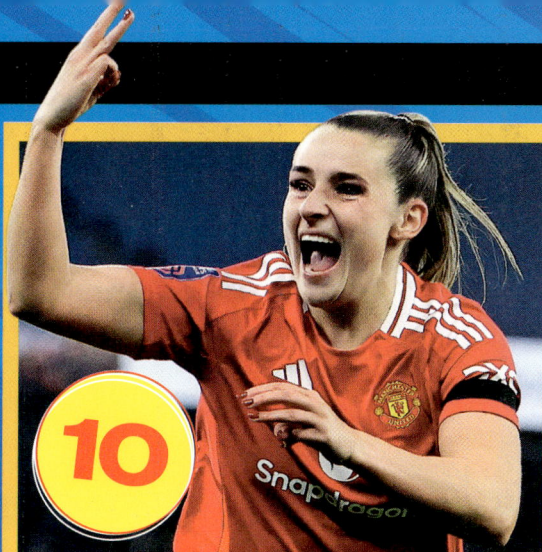

10

COLLAGE CRAFT!

REP A TOP baller with a sick collage. Cut out pics from an old MOTD magazine or print some off — and then stick them all together to create a masterpiece!

COMPLETED IT! ✓

GO TO A NEW STADIUM!

THERE ARE SO many ledge grounds in the UK, from the Prem to non-league. Go check one out!

8

COMPLETED IT! ✓

SOCK SKILLSTER!

11

BALL-UP A pair of your least stinky socks, then use them to practise your tek. Just be super careful not to break anything!

COMPLETED IT! ✓

RATE THE STADIUM SCRAN!

9

HAVE A BITE to eat at the next game you go to. Healthy or unhealthy, tasty or not tasty — let us know your review!

COMPLETED IT! ✓

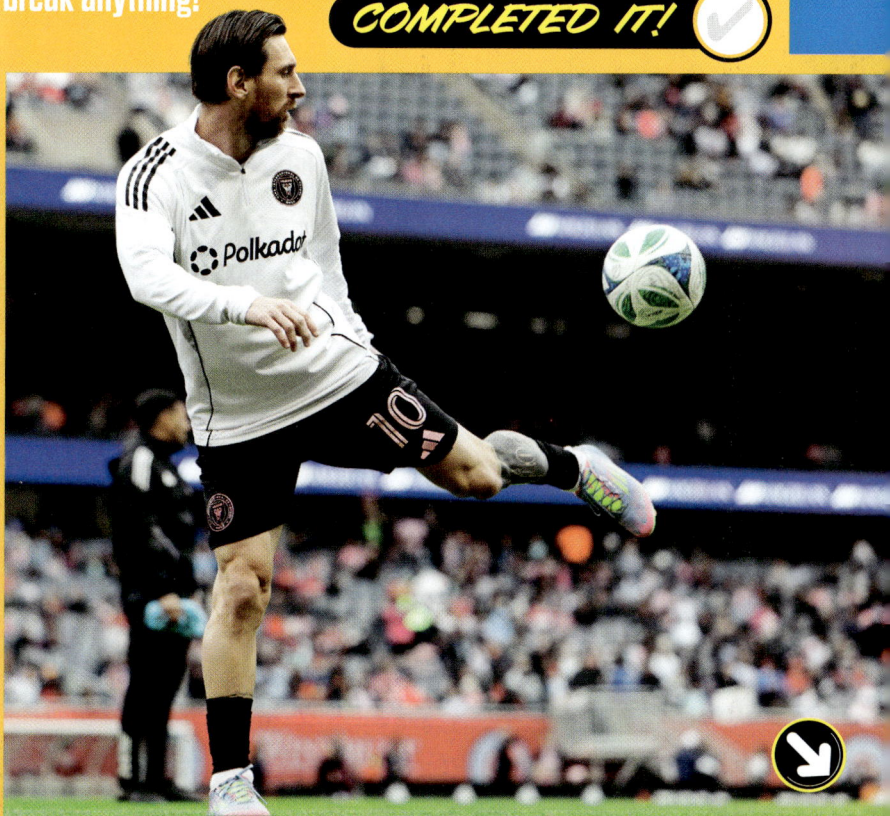

WORLD CLASS!

12 FOLLOW A NEW TEAM!

DO YOU HAVE a Bundesliga team? What about WSL? Pick a club from a different league and learn all about them. You may find a new fave player!

COMPLETED IT! ✔

13 LIVE LIKE A PLAYER!

FROM EATING HEALTHILY to doing your stretches, spend a whole day pretending to be a pro baller. That means some serious training time, too!

COMPLETED IT! ✔

14 BE THE VAR!

WATCH A MATCH — or some Match of the Day highlights — and play referee. Keep an eye out for VAR and make your calls on the penalties and offsides!

COMPLETED IT! ✔

15 BACKHEEL BANTZ!

IT'S TIME TO pull out one of the vibiest moves in footy. Next time you're playing, try and bag an assist, a nutmeg or a goal with a cheeky backheel!

COMPLETED IT! ✔

MASTER A SKILL!

16

NOW LET'S REALLY level up. Spend some time practising one specific move like the Rainbow Flick, Around the World or... whatever this one is!

COMPLETED IT! ✓

SING AT A WSL GAME!

17

THE ATMOS CAN be absolutely top-notch at women's games. Go to one at any level and use your voice. It'll be well fun!

COMPLETED IT! ✓

18

SUPER SELFIE!

GRAB AN EPIC footy selfie — whether that's with a player, mascot, trophy or even your fave programme seller. Happy snapping!

COMPLETED IT! ✓

SO, WHAT IS YOUR LEVEL?

COMPLETE FOUR OR MORE TASKS FROM EACH CATEGORY TO EARN YOUR FINAL RATING. THEN TICK IT HERE!

AMATEUR ✓

PROFESSIONAL ✓

WORLD CLASS ✓

THE BIG PREM PHOTO-WORD!

CAN YOU crush this Premier League photo-word?

HOW TO PLAY
- Use the picture and word clues to complete the crossword.
- Then, collect the letters in the shaded squares to answer the bonus question.

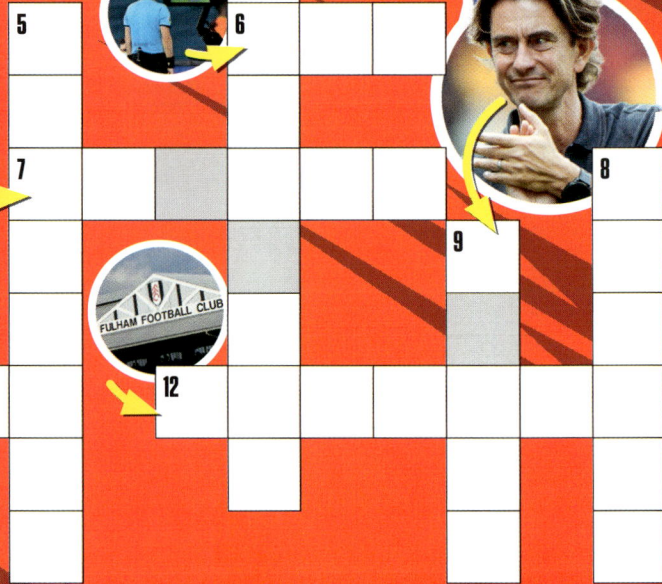

ACROSS
2. Florian's nationality (6)
3. What West Ham blow (7)
6. Tech for refs (1, 1, 1)
7. Surname of French City-zen (6)
11. Man. United captain's first name (5)
12. Craven _____ (7)
13. Surname of England's starboy winger (4)
14. Sweden striker, Alexander _____ (4)

DOWN
1. Brighton's nickname (8)
4. 2024-25 Premier League champs (9)
5. England's No.1, Jordan _____ (8)
8. Booming striker, Jean-Philippe _____ (6)
9. Danish boss, Thomas _____ (5)
10. Official Prem match ball brand (4)
11. Sunderland's nickname (5,4)

ANSWERS ON p92!

BONUS QUESTION! Now collect the letters in the shaded squares. **Rearrange them to spell the surname of a Prem penalty taker!**

44

BRAZIL

128 CAPS

79 GOALS

MATCH OF THE DAY MAGAZINE

REAL O

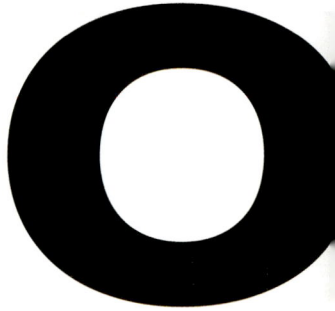

Madame Tussauds unveiled two new footy waxworks in 2025:
'King Kyl' – Kylian Mbappe, and Mary 'Queen of Stops' – Mary Earps!

KYLIAN MBAPPE

Position Striker
Country France

B REAL ☑ WAX ☑

A REAL ☑ WAX ☑

A REAL ☑ WAX ☑

MARY EARPS

Position Goalkeeper
Country England

B REAL ☑ WAX ☑

A REAL ☑ WAX ☑

CRISTIANO

Position Strike

R WAX?

Take a walk down the **MOTD** Madame Tussauds Hall of Fame – work out which footballer is wax and which is the real deal? Tick your choices!

LIONEL MESSI
Position Forward
Country Argentina

MANUEL NEUER
Position Goalkeeper
Country Germany

RONALDO
Country Portugal

B REAL ☐ WAX ☐

A REAL ☐ WAX ☐

B REAL ☐ WAX ☐

A REAL ☐ WAX ☐

B REAL ☐ WAX ☐

✚ **WAX STAT!**
DID YOU KNOW it takes around six months, 500 measurements, 300 photos and 150kg of clay to make just one waxwork figure? Wow!

ANSWERS ON p92!

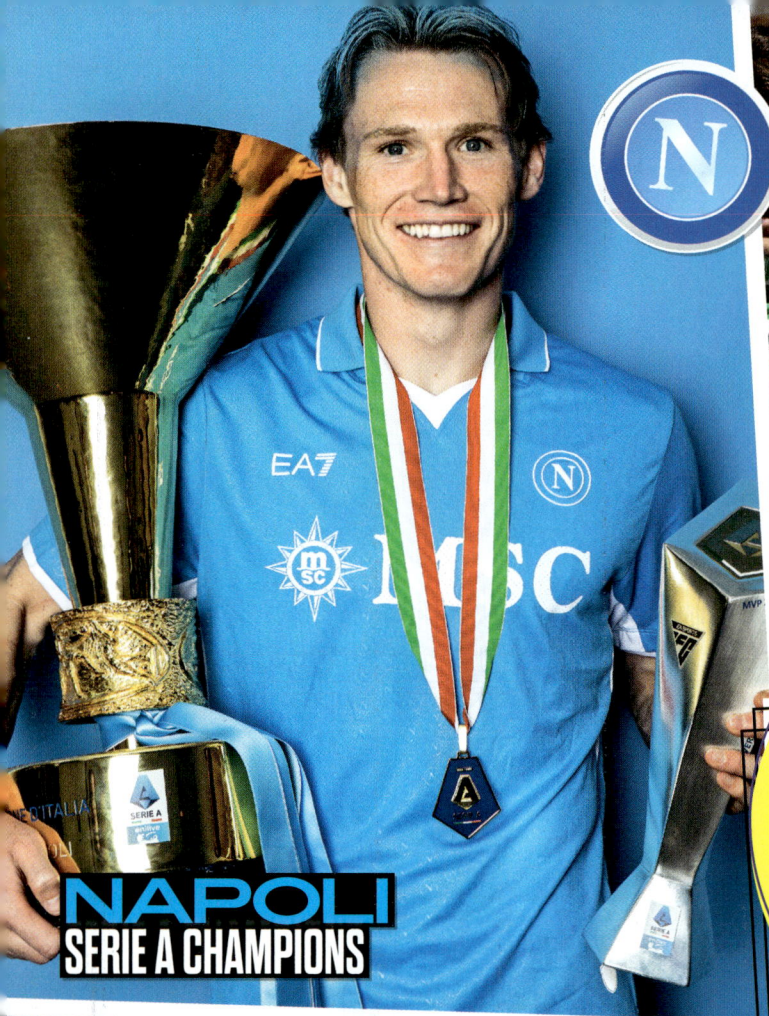

NAPOLI
SERIE A CHAMPIONS

CELTIC
SPFL CHAMPIONS

2024-25

LE
WINN

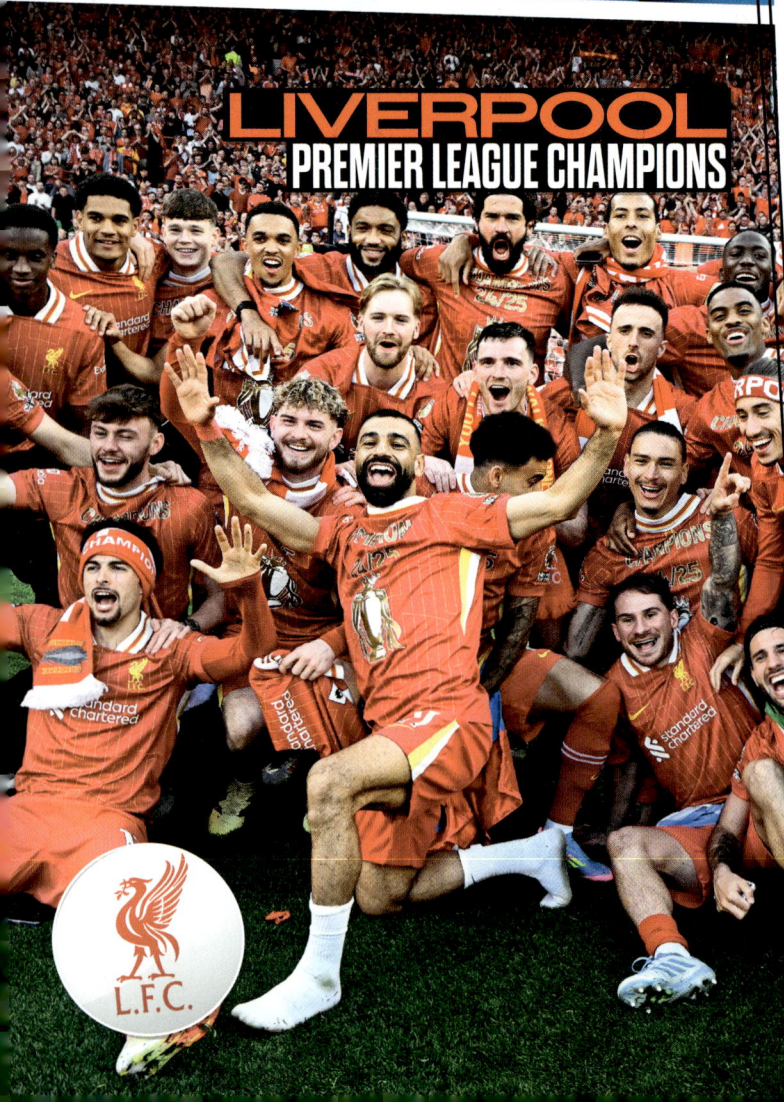

LIVERPOOL
PREMIER LEAGUE CHAMPIONS

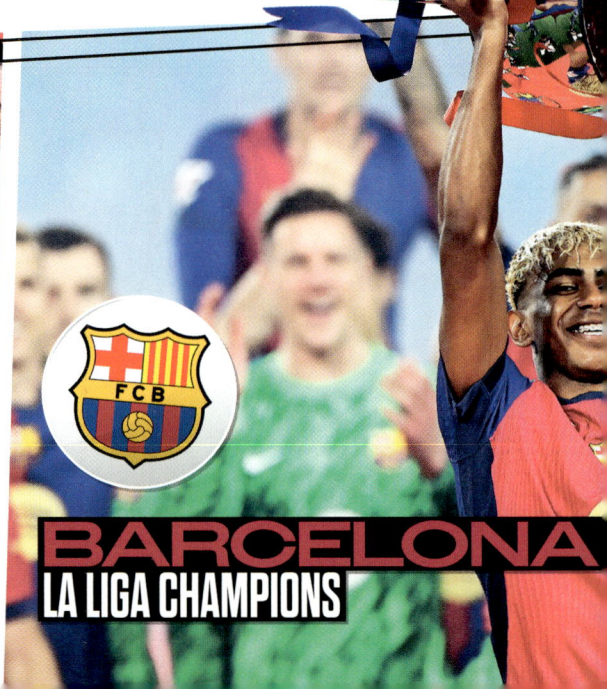

BARCELONA
LA LIGA CHAMPIONS

BAYERN MUNICH
BUNDESLIGA CHAMPIONS

AGUE
ERS!

CHAMPIONS 2025
LIGUE 1

PSG
LIGUE 1 CHAMPIONS

WOMEN'S SUPER LEAGUE
CHAMPIONS
2024-25

CHELSEA WOMEN
WSL CHAMPIONS

Alessia

RUSSO

England

51 CAPS

23 GOALS

GOAL QUEEN!

BBC MATCH OF THE DAY MAGAZINE

THE A-Z OF THE WORLD CUP!

More squads, more stars — the 2026 World Cup will be the biggest ever!

Get ready with our guide to the **greatest tournament** on the planet...

A is for... ANCELOTTI'S EYEBROW!

THE MOST famous eyebrow in football will be at the World Cup — for Brazil! Super-successful coach Carlo Ancelotti has ONE mission as boss of Brazil — to help them win their first World Cup since 2002. Will he be lifting the trophy... or just that eyebrow?

WORLD CUP Q
Which two other countries have won back-to-back World Cups?

[   ] and [   ]

B is for... BACK-TO-BACK!

ARGENTINA ARE the reigning world champions — and they have a new aim — to become just the third nation in World Cup history to win back-to-back tournaments. Can they crack it? All eyes will be on Lionel Messi & Co.!

C is for... CELES!

PLAYING AT the World Cup? Prep your best cele! These players crushed it in the past — and we can't wait to see who brings a standout celebration in 2026!

Antoine Griezmann's Fortnite-inspired cele went global in 2018

Ecuador forward Ivan Kaviedes spun this Spider-Man mask cele in 2006

Brazil brought the samba dancing — and the goals in 2022

Cameroon hero Roger Milla's famous dance at Italia '90

D is for... DODGY DOs!

MOHAWKS, MULLETS, man-buns... the World Cup is a stage for the most iconic — and awful hair styles. Who will be the hair-oes in 2026?

Ronaldo's World Cup winning haircut in 2002. Kids copied the style and R9 later apologised — he even said his Mum hated it

E is for... ESTADIO AZTECA!

THE 2026 World Cup kicks off at the epic Estadio Azteca in Mexico City. At 2,200m above sea level, this is one of the highest altitude stadiums in the world. It has history too — two footy legends — Pele and Diego Maradona — both won World Cups here!

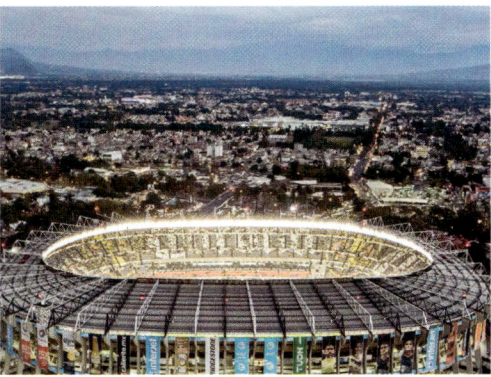

F is for... FANS!

BIG WIGS, face paint, hero masks and mad outfits — footy fans love to go all out at a World Cup! In 2026, a record five million fans will attend matches and six billion will tune in worldwide!

G is for... GOAT GOALS!

THEY GO AGAIN! Lionel Messi and Cristiano Ronaldo will be at their record-breaking sixth World Cup! Messi is on two more missions — net four goals to become the tournament's all-time top scorer and to be at his brilliant best to win the Golden Ball for a record third time!

H is for... HOST NATIONS!

CANADA

USA

MEXICO

FOR THE first time ever, there are three host nations. Sixteen cities across the USA, Mexico and Canada will host 48 teams and 104 games. Due to the distance and four different time zones, teams will play group games in the same region — East, Central or West. Phew!

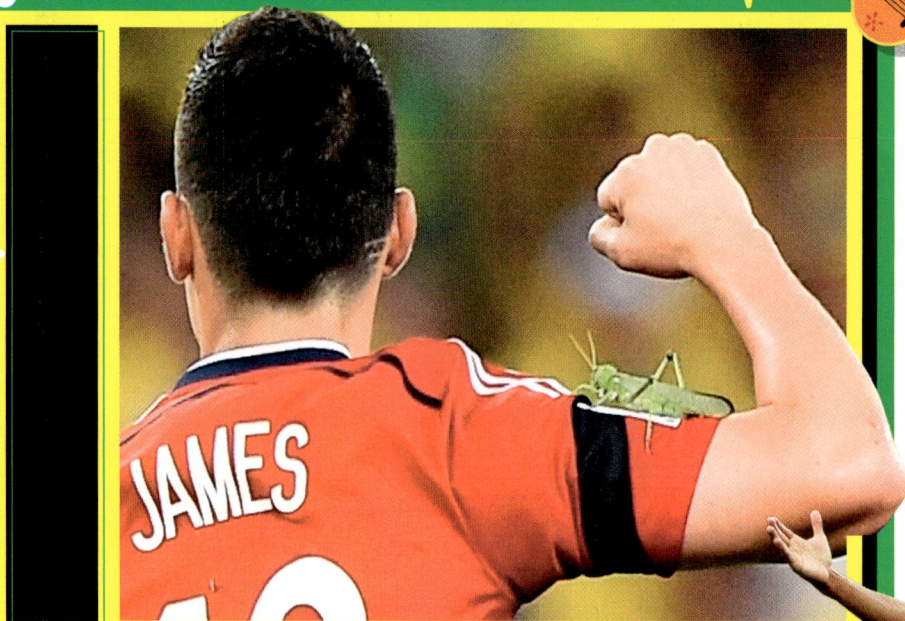

I is for...
INSECT ATTACKS!

PLAYERS SHOULD prep for another threat on the pitch — insects! Bugs have crawled into World Cup history — Harry Maguire battled midges in Russia 2018, while Colombia's James Rodriguez carried a grasshopper four years earlier!

J is for...
JUUUDE!

WHO ELSE? Jude Bellingham is just made for the big stage. At 19, he bagged on his World Cup debut in Qatar. At Euro 2024, he saved England with that overhead kick. Fast forward to summer 2026 — what's Jude gonna do?

K is for...
KITS!

SOME ARE iconic, others are eyesores — but a World Cup means new national kits. Prepare to rate — and hate — the new 2026 drops!

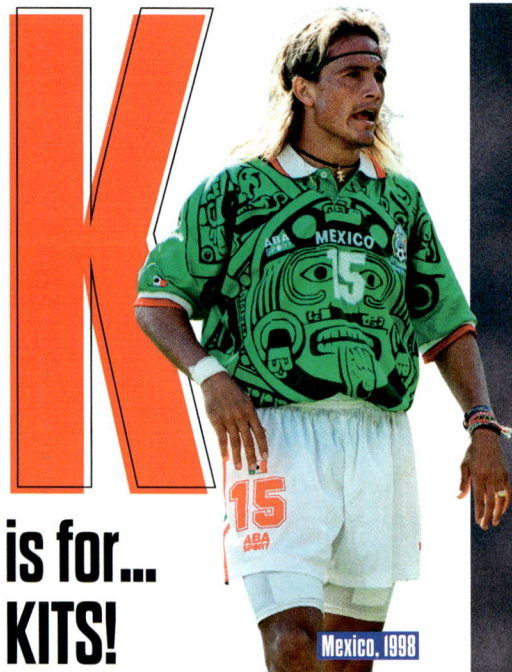

Mexico, 1998

Germany, 1990

L is for... LIMPING OFF!

BUBBLE-WRAP your best ballers now — no-one wants an injury in a World Cup year. But even worse, don't get clattered in a quarter-final in your home country. Brazil's star player Neymar sent the country into a state of mourning after he was stretchered off in 2014!

M is for... MASCOTS!

A LION, a dog, an armadillo, a rooster, an orange in full kit and a chilli pepper with a moustache! The World Cup has a history of wild, wacky and totally weird mascots!

DRAW A MASCOT FOR THE 2026 WORLD CUP

The host nations are USA, Mexico and Canada!

N is for... NEW YORK!

THIS WORLD CUP kicks off in Mexico, but the final will be in New York. The Metlife stadium is usually home to two NFL teams — the New York Giants and the New York Jets, but for the first time, it will host a World Cup Final complete with a half-time show — just like the Super Bowl!

METLIFE STADIUM

WORLD CUP Q

Which music star would YOU pick to perform at the World Cup Final?

O is for... ONE GOAL!

HOST NATION Canada have only ever scored one goal in their World Cup history — bagged by Bayern Munich left-back Alphonso Davies in 2022. The Maple Leafs will be looking to double or triple it in 2026!

Q is for... QUESADILLAS!

MEXICAN FOOTBALL stadiums have some of the best footy scran on the planet — fans at this World Cup will be chomping through tacos, corn on the cobs and yummy quesadillas — a tasty little cheesy wrap!

P is for... PENALTY SHOOTOUTS!

BACK IN 1994, when the USA last hosted the tourney, the World Cup Final was decided on penalties for the very first time. Italy's brilliant baller Roberto Baggio blazed the final penalty kick over the bar — handing the trophy to Brazil. It still haunts their hero today (as does that ponytail!)

Roberto Baggio skied the final penalty in 1994

WORLD CUP Q

Can you translate these US footy expressions?

"Oh, nice soccer cleats!"

"Woah — he's hit that upper 90!"

"The keeper had a shutout!"

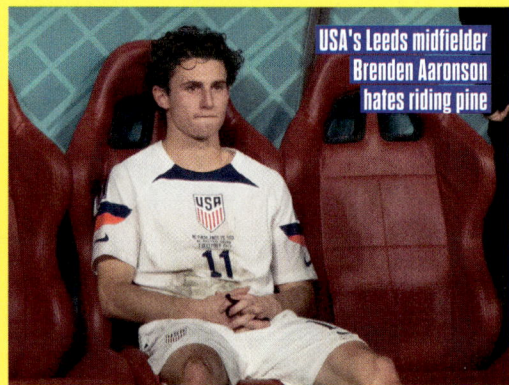

USA's Leeds midfielder Brenden Aaronson hates riding pine

R is for... RIDING PINE!

THE GAME is the same — but US footy lingo isn't! Expect to hear different footy phrases — such as 'riding pine'. It comes from baseball and American commentators use it when a player is sitting on the bench!

ANSWERS: 1 Soccer cleats = football boots; 2 Shutout = clean sheet; 3 Upper 90 = top corner

56

S is for... STICKERS!

GOT, GOT, NEED! We love the tournament tradition of unpacking a set of stickers — spotting a superstar, a shiny badge and a Slovenian player you've never heard of — and swapping them with your mates!

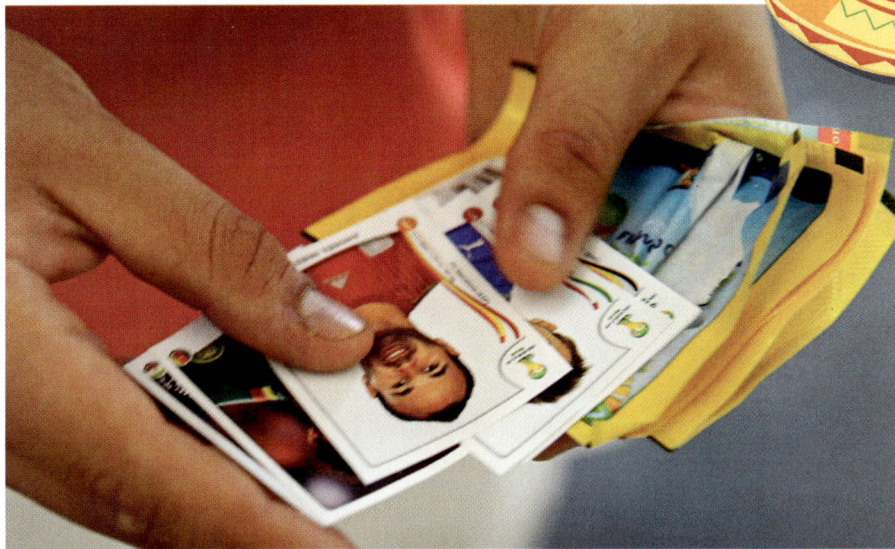

T is for... TUCHEL TIME!

IT WILL be 60 years since England won the World Cup — beating West Germany in 1966. Can the Three Lions finally lift it again with a German coach? With Thomas Tuchel on tactics, fresh new talent AND all-time top-scorer Harry Kane — expectations are high!

U is for... UZBEKISTAN!

YOU MAY not be able to find this country on a map — but you WILL find them at the 2026 World Cup. That's because they are the first Central Asian country to ever qualify for the tournament in its 96-year history. Up the Uzbeks!

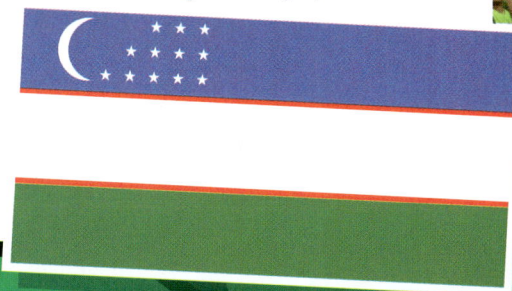

Man. City defender Abdukodir Khusanov balls for Uzbekistan

V is for... VILLAINS!

FOR EVERY World Cup hero, there's a villain — the foulest of footballers who has a moment of madness! From Diego Maradona's 'Hand of God' goal for Argentina against England in 1986 to Luis Suarez's shoulder chomp on Giorgio Chiellini in 2014 — it's not the spirit, but it adds to the drama!

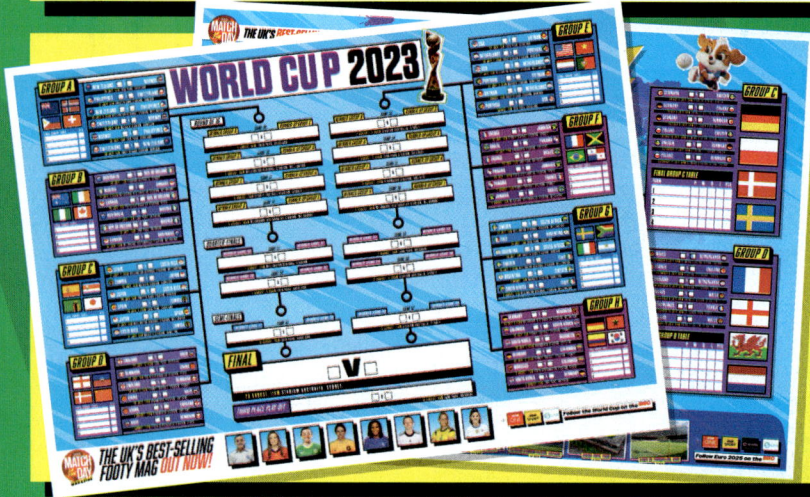

W is for... WALLCHARTS!

SHARPEN YOUR pencils and make space on your wall. With 16 extra nations — and a total of 104 games, the MOTD magazine 2026 World Cup wallchart is going to be a whopper!

X is for... xG*!

*EXPECTED GOALS

THERE WERE a record-breaking 172 goals at the 2022 World Cup — but with extra games and new teams — the expected number of goals in 2026 will be off the scale!

WORLD CUP PREDICTION

Who will be top scorer in 2026?

Y

is for...
YOUNG TEK!

THREE OF THE world's tekkiest talents are set for their first World Cup in 2026 — and we can't wait. Get hyped for Spain's Lamine Yamal, France's Champions League winner Desire Doue, and Real Madrid's Argentinian attacker, Franco Mastantuono!

Z

is for...
ZINGERS!

AND Z is what the World Cup is all about! Those breath-taking moments of magic when the ball is blasted into the net — stunning the oppo — and sending entire nations into raptures. Bring it on!

WSL REWIND!

ANSWERS ON p92!

I POINT for each correct answer!

Can you name all nine of these baby-faced **WSL** ballers?

1
A Keira Walsh
B Fran Kirby
C Guro Reiten

2
A Kim Little
B Ella Toone
C Katie McCabe

3
A Chloe Kelly
B Laura Coombs
C Alex Greenwood

4
A Erin Cuthbert
B Vivianne Miedema
C Lucy Bronze

5
A Hannah Hampton
B Lauren Hemp
C Missy Bo Kearns

6
A Leah Williamson
B Beth Mead
C Alessia Russo

7
A Aggie Beever-Jones
B Millie Bright
C Bethany England

8
A Stina Blackstenius
B Rachel Daly
C Leah Galton

9
A Khadija Shaw
B Nikita Parris
C Khiara Keating

YOUR FOOTY BRAIN POWER

YOUR SCORE ☐ /9

9	GENIUS
7	PROFESSIONAL
5	SEMI-PRO
3	AMATEUR
1	SUNDAY LEAGUE
0	OH NO, DISASTER

DREAM

PAST, PRESENT

BRASIL

10

TEAMS

AND FUTURE!

Football is **STACKED** with superstars right now, but how does this current crop of ballers compare to football icons of the past and the next generation of rising stars? Well, let's find out! We've put three ultimate line-ups together – which is your favourite?

DREAM TEAM 1

FROM THE PAST!

Here's our legendary line-up made up of the best players from footy history!

GK

GIANLUIGI BUFFON
Main club: Juventus
Years active: 1995-2023
Country: Italy

RB

CAFU
Main club: AC Milan
Years active: 1989-2008
Country: Brazil

CB

BOBBY MOORE
Main club: West Ham
Years active: 1958-1978
Country: England

CB

FRANZ BECKENBAUER
Main club: Bayern Munich
Years active: 1964-1983
Country: Germany

LB

PAOLO MALDINI
Main club: AC Milan
Years active: 1984-2009
Country: Italy

CM

LOTHAR MATTHAUS
Main club: Bayern Munich
Years active: 1978-2000
Country: Germany

CM

ZINEDINE ZIDANE

Main club: Real Madrid
Years active: 1989-2006
Country: France

LW

DIEGO MARADONA

Main club: Napoli
Years active: 1976-1997
Country: Argentina

RW

LIONEL MESSI

Main club: Barcelona
Years active: 2004-present
Country: Argentina

ST

PELE

Main club: Santos
Years active: 1956-1977
Country: Brazil

ST

CRISTIANO RONALDO

Main club: Real Madrid
Years active: 2002-present
Country: Portugal

DRAW THEM A KIT!

BUFFON

CAFU

MOORE   BECKENBAUER

MALDINI

MATTHAUS   ZIDANE

MESSI

PELE   RONALDO

MARADONA

MANAGER

SIR ALEX FERGUSON

Main club: Man. United
Years active: 1974-2013
Country: Scotland

SUPER SUB

JOHAN CRUYFF

Main club: Ajax
Years active: 1964-1984
Country: Netherlands

DREAM TEAM 2

FROM THE PRESENT!

Here's our ultimate XI of the best ballers in the world right now!

GK
THIBAUT COURTOIS
Club: Real Madrid   **Age:** 33
Country: Belgium

RB
TRENT ALEXANDER-ARNOLD
Club: Real Madrid   **Age:** 26
Country: England

CB
VIRGIL VAN DIJK
Club: Liverpool   **Age:** 34
Country: Netherlands

CB
ALESSANDRO BASTONI
Club: Inter Milan   **Age:** 26
Country: Italy

LB
NUNO MENDES
Club: PSG   **Age:** 23
Country: Portugal

CDM
RODRI
Club: Man. City   **Age:** 29
Country: Spain

CM
JUDE BELLINGHAM
Club: Real Madrid **Age:** 22
Country: England

CM
PEDRI
Club: Barcelona **Age:** 22
Country: Spain

RW
MOHAMED SALAH
Club: Liverpool **Age:** 33
Country: Egypt

ST
KYLIAN MBAPPE
Club: Real Madrid **Age:** 26
Country: France

LW
VINICIUS JR
Club: Real Madrid **Age:** 25
Country: Brazil

DRAW THEM A KIT!

COURTOIS

ALEXANDER-ARNOLD

VAN DIJK

BASTONI

MENDES

PEDRI

RODRI

BELLINGHAM

SALAH

VINICIUS JR

MBAPPE

MANAGER
CARLO ANCELOTTI
Current team: Brazil
Age: 66 **Country:** Italy

SUPER SUB
ERLING HAALAND
Club: Man. City **Age:** 25
Country: Norway

DREAM TEAM 3

FROM THE FUTURE!

Here's our team of the next-gen GOATs you need to know about!

GK
MIKE PENDERS
Club: Chelsea **Age:** 20
Country: Belgium

RB
JOSH ACHEAMPONG
Club: Chelsea **Age:** 19
Country: England

CB
VITOR REIS
Club: Man. City **Age:** 19
Country: Brazil

CB
PAU CUBARSI
Club: Barcelona **Age:** 18
Country: Spain

LB
MYLES LEWIS-SKELLY
Club: Arsenal **Age:** 18
Country: England

CM
JOAO NEVES
Club: PSG **Age:** 20
Country: Portugal

CM

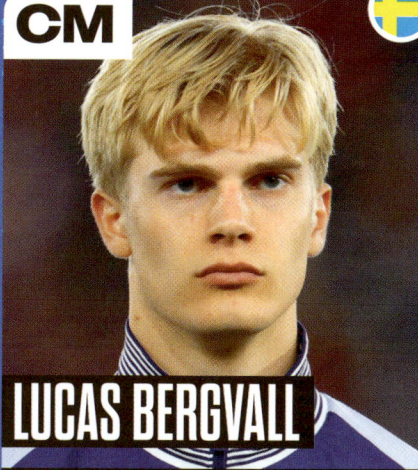

LUCAS BERGVALL

Club: Tottenham **Age:** 19
Country: Sweden

CAM

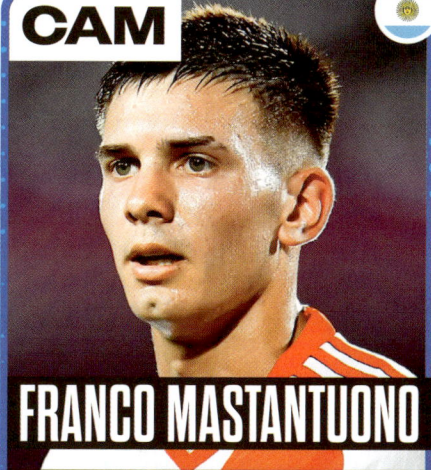

FRANCO MASTANTUONO

Club: Real Madrid **Age:** 18
Country: Argentina

RW

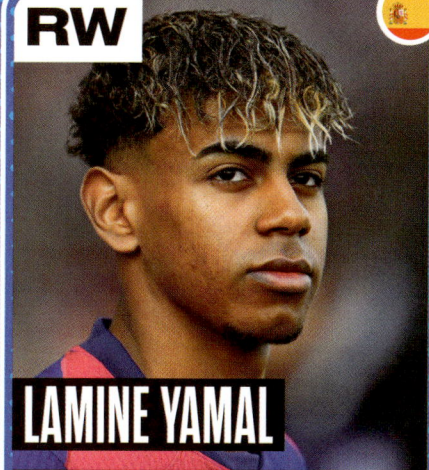

LAMINE YAMAL

Club: Barcelona **Age:** 18
Country: Spain

ST

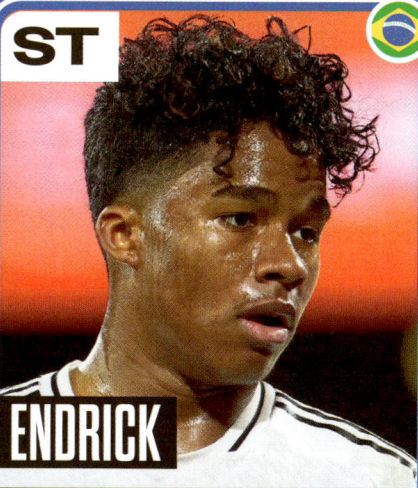

ENDRICK

Club: Real Madrid **Age:** 19
Country: Brazil

LW

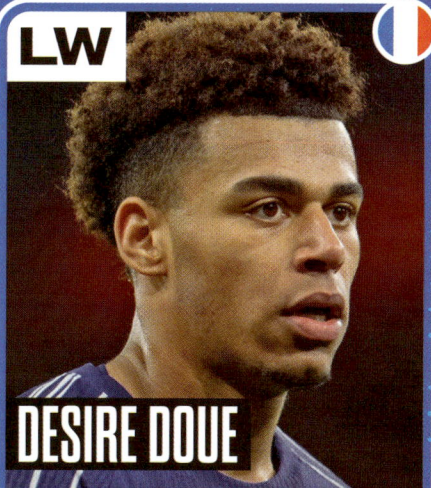

DESIRE DOUE

Club: PSG **Age:** 20
Country: France

DRAW THEM A KIT!

PENDERS

ACHEAMPONG
REIS
CUBARSI
LEWIS-SKELLY
BERGVALL
NEVES
YAMAL
MASTANTUONO
DOUE
ENDRICK

MANAGER

FABIAN HURZELER

Club: Brighton **Age:** 32
Country: Germany

SUPER SUB

ESTEVAO WILLIAN

Club: Chelsea **Age:** 18
Country: Brazil

69

GOAL QUEEN!

VIVIANNE MIEDEMA

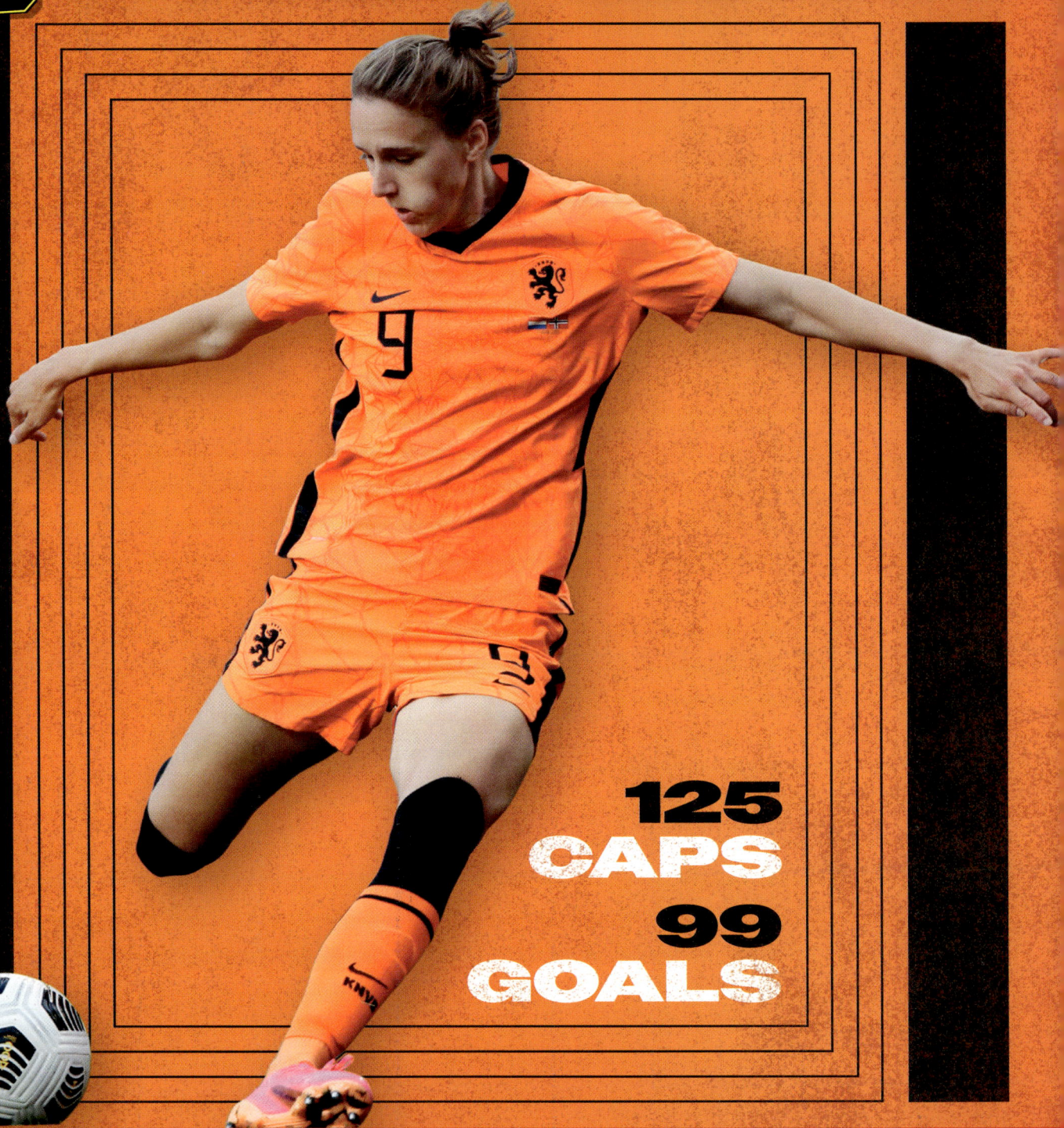

125 CAPS

99 GOALS

NETHERLANDS

THE 5-A-SIDE BATTLE!

We've picked the ultimate mini-team from each top Euro league — but how do you rate them?

PREMIER LEAGUE

- Alisson — LIVERPOOL
- Virgil van Dijk — LIVERPOOL
- Rodri — MAN. CITY
- Mohamed Salah — LIVERPOOL
- Erling Haaland — MAN. CITY

LA LIGA

- Thibaut Courtois — REAL MADRID
- Antonio Rudiger — REAL MADRID
- Jude Bellingham — REAL MADRID
- Lamine Yamal — BARCELONA
- Kylian Mbappe — REAL MADRID

LIGUE 1

- Gianluigi Donnarumma — PSG
- Achraf Hakimi — PSG
- Paul Pogba — MONACO
- Ousmane Dembele — PSG
- Khvicha Kvaratskhelia — PSG

SERIE A

- David De Gea — FIORENTINA
- Alessandro Bastoni — INTER MILAN
- Kevin De Bruyne — NAPOLI
- Rafael Leao — AC MILAN
- Lautaro Martinez — INTER MILAN

BUNDESLIGA

- Gregor Kobel — BORUSSIA DORTMUND
- Alejandro Grimaldo — BAYER LEVERKUSEN
- Jamal Musiala — BAYERN MUNICH
- Michael Olise — BAYERN MUNICH
- Harry Kane — BAYERN MUNICH

THE TEAMS RANKED!

Put these teams in order of how good you think they are — with the best team at No.1!

1 ....
2 ....
3 ....
4 ....
5 ....

71

SON

Heung-min

SOUTH KOREA

134 CAPS

51 GOALS

GOAL KING!

KIDS' QUIZ!

I POINT for each correct answer!

1
WHICH SAUDI PRO LEAGUE TEAM DOES CRISTIANO RONALDO PLAY FOR?

A Al Ahli ☑ **B** Al Hilal ☑ **C** Al Nassr ☑ **D** Al Qadsiah ☑

2
WHICH OF THESE PLAYERS WON THE 2025 CHAMPIONS LEAGUE?

A Jude Bellingham ☑ **B** Ousmane Dembele ☑

C Phil Foden ☑ **D** Harry Kane ☑

3

WHICH CURRENT PREM STAR IS PICTURED HERE IN THIS OLD PHOTO?

A Jarrod Bowen ☑
B Erling Haaland ☑
C Anthony Gordon ☑
D Martin Odegaard ☑

4

THIS IS THE FLAG OF A COUNTRY THAT PLAYED AT EURO 2025 – CAN YOU NAME THAT NATION?

A France ☑ **B** Germany ☑
C Spain ☑ **D** Portugal ☑

5
WHICH OF THESE EPIC TROPHIES IS THE FA CUP?

A ☑ **B** ☑

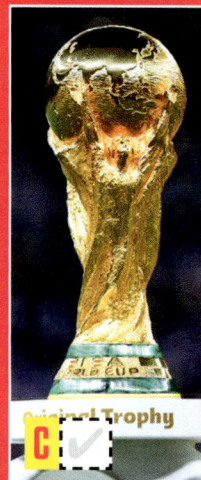 

C ☑ **D** ☑

6. WHICH LIONESS HAS PLAYED MORE THAN 100 TIMES FOR ENGLAND?

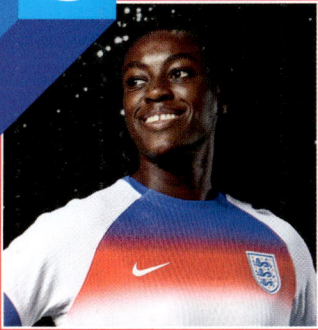
A Michelle Agyemang

B Niamh Charles

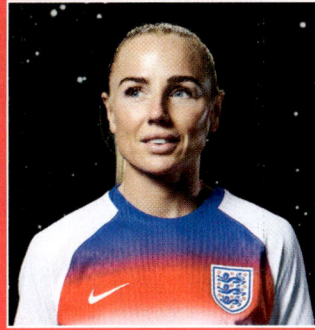
C Alex Greenwood

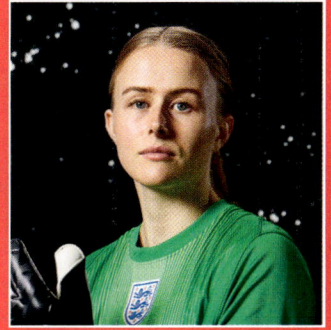
D Hannah Hampton

7. THIS DUDE IS THE MASCOT OF WHICH PREM CLUB?

A Burnley
B Leeds
C Sunderland
D West Ham

8. CHELSEA SIGNED STRIKER LIAM DELAP FROM WHICH CLUB?

A Coventry
B Southampton
C Derby
D Ipswich

9. ENGLAND MEN'S TEAM IS KNOWN AS THE...

A Two Rhinos

B Three Lions

C Four Tigers

D Five Parrots

10. WHICH OF THESE CLUBS PLAYS IN THE BUNDESLIGA?

A Benfica

B Fiorentina

C Valencia

D Werder Bremen

TURN TO PAGE 92 FOR THE ANSWERS!

HOW DID YOU DO? ☐ /10

ADULTS' QUIZ!

You got this!

1

WHICH OF THESE CLUBS DID **NICOLAS ANELKA** NEVER PLAY FOR?

A Bolton

B Inter Milan

C Juventus

D PSG

2

WHICH OF THESE ICONS FINISHED AS TOP SCORER AT THE **2006 WORLD CUP?**

A Hernan Crespo

B Miroslav Klose

C Ronaldo

D Zinedine Zidane

3

NAME THE LEGENDARY **LIONESS** CHATTING WITH **PRINCE WILLIAM!**

A Lucy Bronze

B Steph Houghton

C Jill Scott

D Rachel Yankey

4

2003 BALLON D'OR WINNER **PAVEL NEDVED** PLAYED FOR WHICH COUNTRY?

A Serbia

B Czech Republic

C Croatia

D Romania

5

IN WHICH COUNTRY WOULD YOU FIND THE **BOMBONERA?**

A Argentina

B Italy

C Brazil

D Mexico

6 WHO WON GOAL OF THE SEASON IN 2000 FOR HIS SCISSOR-VOLLEY?

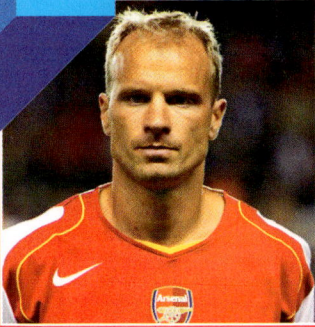
A Dennis Bergkamp

B Paolo Di Canio

C Erik Lamela

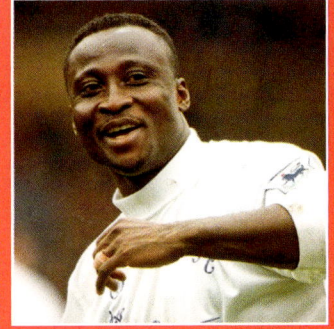
D Tony Yeboah

7

NAME THE ICONIC ENGLAND CAPTAIN HOLDING BRIGHTON MASCOT, TIDDLES THE CAT!

A Jimmy Arfield
B Bobby Moore
C Johnny Haynes
D Billy Wright

8

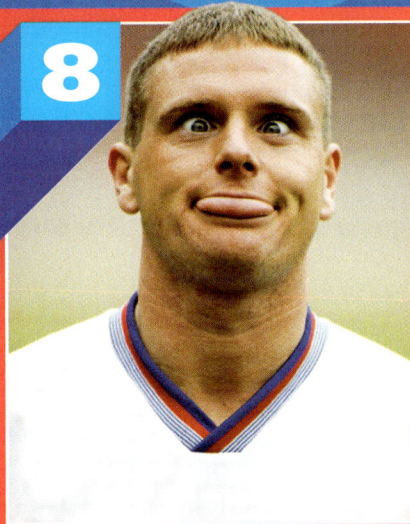

PAUL GASCOIGNE WON TWO DOMESTIC LEAGUE TITLES WITH WHICH CLUB?

A Everton
B Lazio
C Newcastle
D Rangers

9 FINISH THE NAME OF THE AMERICAN TEAM PELE PLAYED FOR. NEW YORK...

A Cosmos

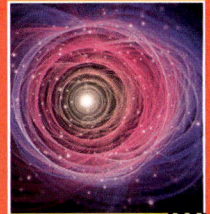
B Galaxy

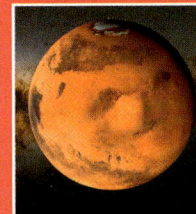
C Mars

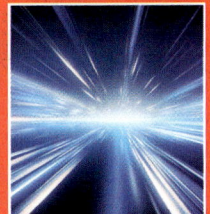
D Universe

10 WHICH CLUB WON THE FIRST-EVER WOMEN'S SUPER LEAGUE BACK IN 2011?

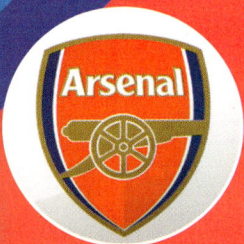
A Arsenal

B Birmingham

C Chelsea

D Doncaster

TURN TO PAGE 92 FOR THE ANSWERS!

HOW DID THEY DO? ☐ /10

6 MISS!

3 GOAL!

2 GOAL!

1 GOAL!

PENALTY SHOOTO

HOW TO PLAY!

1 Grab a dice and a mate and you're ready to go — both roll the dice and whoever gets the higher number goes first.

2 Player 1 rolls the dice — the number it lands on decides where your penalty goes. Then it's Player 2's turn.

3 Each player gets five rolls and whoever scores the most, wins. Keep count of the score on the scoreboard on p79 — if it's level after five pens, it's sudden death. Good luck!

THE SCOREBOARD

Each time you take a pen, put a mark in the box — whoever has scored the most after five penalties, wins!

✔ = GOAL!
✗ = MISS!

5 MISS!

4 MISS!

CAN YOU HANDLE THE PRESSURE?

UT GAME!

Are you deadly from 12 yards or will you crumble and scuff it wide? It's time for the most nerve-wracking thing in footy — the dreaded penalty shootout! Eek!

PLAYER 1		
PENALTY 1	☐	☐
PENALTY 2	☐	☐
PENALTY 3	☐	☐
PENALTY 4	☐	☐
PENALTY 5	☐	☐
FINAL SCORE	☐	

PLAYER 2		
PENALTY 1	☐	☐
PENALTY 2	☐	☐
PENALTY 3	☐	☐
PENALTY 4	☐	☐
PENALTY 5	☐	☐
FINAL SCORE	☐	

ROBERT LEWANDOWSKI

POLAND

158 CAPS
85 GOALS

GOAL KING!

THE TOP 10 TIFOS!

What is a tifo?

'Tifo' comes from the Italian word 'tifoso' which means 'fan'. Tifos are giant flags or colourful mosaic pictures displayed in the stands by fans. They show their support for the team, oh, and they look epic, too!

TURN OVER FOR TEN TIFOS!

10 CENTURY AT SELHURST!

WHO? Crystal Palace **WHERE?** Selhurst Park, London, England
WHAT? Eagles superfans celebrated 100 years of Selhurst Park with this tifo in 2024

9 TOON TIFOS!

WHO? Newcastle
WHERE? St. James' Park, Newcastle, England
WHAT? The Toon Army pulled out these giant tifos to celebrate their heroes Anthony Gordon, Alexander Isak and manager Eddie Howe

NEWCASTLE UNITED

GORDON 10

SELA.SA/NUFC

XANDER THE GREAT

WE'RE NOT HERE TO BE POPULAR, WE'RE HERE TO COMPET

A CITY, A CLUB, A HISTORY!

WHO? Marseille
WHERE? Stade Velodrome, Marseille, France
WHAT? Marseille fans are mega proud of their club and city. In 2024, they celebrated the 125th anniversary of the club with this mega tifo, which shows the city of Marseille

CELTIC CELES!

WHO? Celtic
WHERE? Celtic Park, Glasgow, Scotland
WHAT? Celtic have a tradition for tifos with a religious, social or political message. The Bhoys bring out their best for the Old Firm clash — the derby game against Rangers

6 LOS VIKINGOS!

WHO? Real Madrid **WHERE?** Bernabeu, Madrid, Spain
WHAT? Did you know Real Madrid are also nicknamed the Vikings?
That's why you may spot Viking helmets and a Viking tifo at the Bernabeu

5 ROAR-SOME RETURN!

WHO? Aston Villa **WHERE?** Villa Park, Birmingham, England
WHAT? Villa fans roared on their team during their 2024-25 Champions League
campaign with a tifo showing the club's symbol — the rampant lion

4 MUNICH MEMORIES!

WHO? Bayern Munich **WHERE?** Allianz Arena, Munich, Germany **WHAT?** This tifo celebrates the life of a German football legend — defender, captain and coach Franz Beckenbauer, who died in 2024

3 THE SAN SIRO SATAN!

WHO? AC Milan **WHERE?** San Siro, Milan, Italy
WHAT? Don't mess with the Red & Black half of Milan! Their nickname is Il Diavolo, which means The Devil

THE JOURNEY!

WHO? Borussia Dortmund
WHERE? Westfalenstadion, Dortmund, Germany
WHAT? Dortmund's Yellow Wall is world famous. This tifo says: "And every time it's worth standing by your side... this journey will continue forever!"

TROPHY HUNT!

WHO? Borussia Dortmund
WHERE? Westfalenstadion, Dortmund, Germany
WHAT? One of the all-time iconic tifos! This supersized sinister character was looking for 'lost' silverware before a UCL clash in 2013

WIN, WE WILL!

WHO? PSG
WHERE? Parc des Princes, Paris, France
WHAT? This epic Star Wars tifo was unveiled when PSG played Barcelona in 2024. What started as a Darth Vader in Barca colours transformed into a Jedi master — Yoda in PSG shirt

TIFO TIME!

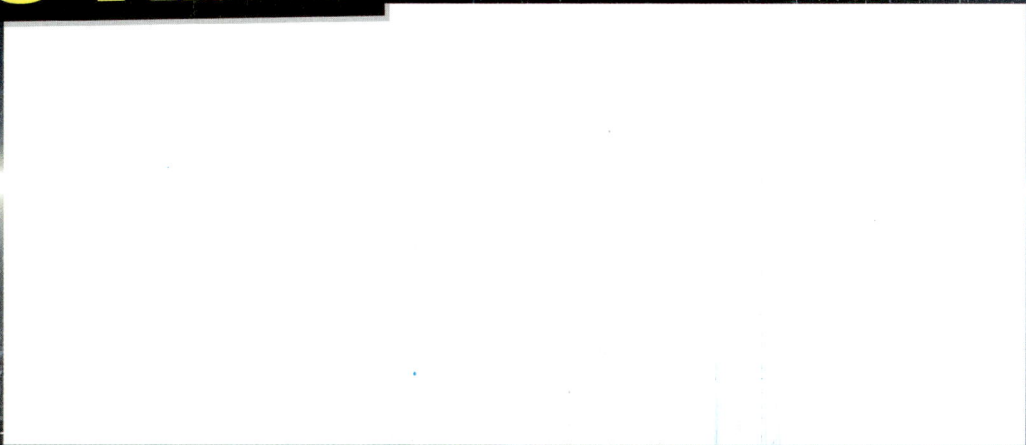

NOW IT'S YOUR TURN! Design a tifo for YOUR club. It could celebrate an amazing player, moment or manager. Think about your club's badge, colours, heroes and history. Then, draw your idea above!

TOP 10

UEFA women's CHAMPIONS LEAGUE®

UWCL STARS!

WE COUNT DOWN the ten best ballers competing in this season's Women's Champions League — but who's No.1?

10

+ KLARA BUHL

CLUB: Bayern Munich
POSITION: Winger
COUNTRY: Germany 🇩🇪
AGE: 24

THE BHUL-DOZER is flattening oppo defences like they're not even there! Klara is queen of creating and is one of the deadliest dribblers around. She topped the charts for assists in the Frauen-Bundesliga last season and secured her third top division title — all at 24!

9

+ LAUREN JAMES

CLUB: Chelsea
POSITION: Forward
COUNTRY: England 🏴󠁧󠁢󠁥󠁮󠁧󠁿
AGE: 23

LJ FEELS like a superstar! The Blues baller is made for the biggest stage — her quick feet, powerful running and silky skills are too hot to handle. The best bit? She's only 23 and although last season was injury hit, we know she's got the tek to light up the WSL and UWCL this campaign!

8

ALESSIA RUSSO

CLUB: Arsenal
POSITION: Striker
COUNTRY: England 🏴󠁧󠁢󠁥󠁮󠁧󠁿
AGE: 26

LESS HAS levelled up! The Arsenal attacker had a 2025 to remember — she was joint-top WSL scorer, was named FWA Women's Footballer of the Year, she scored in the Euros final — oh, and she won the Women's Champions League for the first time. Wow!

7

ALEXIA PUTELLAS

CLUB: Barcelona
POSITION: Midfielder
COUNTRY: Spain 🇪🇸
AGE: 31

YOU'RE LOOKING at a certified legend of the women's game! Lex has been bossing things at Barca for well over ten years, and she isn't slowing down any time soon. Putellas runs the midfield — she's a tidy technician and loves to get in on the goals too!

6

NAOMI GIRMA

CLUB: Chelsea
POSITION: Centre-back
COUNTRY: USA 🇺🇸
AGE: 25

GOOD LUCK getting past Girma! Naomi is the best defender in the game, which is why Chelsea broke the women's transfer record to bring her to Stamford Bridge back in January. She's already picked up two trophies in blue and there'll be loads more to come!

5

SALMA PARALLUELO

CLUB: Barcelona
POSITION: Forward
COUNTRY: Spain
AGE: 21

THERE AREN'T many speedier stars in world football than this lightning-fast forward. The youngster is one of football's most exciting entertainers — she came third in the 2023 and 2024 Ballon d'Or and the top prize could be hers if she keeps up her form!

4

MARIE-ANTOINETTE KATOTO

CLUB: Lyon
POSITION: Striker
COUNTRY: France
AGE: 26

DID YOU know that Marie-Antoinette was the name of the last queen of France? Well, this Marie-Antoinette is the queen of goals. She's the world's deadliest finisher right now and made a big summer switch from PSG to Premiere Ligue rivals Lyon!

3

MARIONA CALDENTEY

CLUB: Arsenal
POSITION: Midfielder
COUNTRY: Spain
AGE: 29

DEBUT SEASONS don't come much better than Mariona's magic first year at Arsenal. She had big boots to fill as a replacement for Gunners' ledge Vivianne Miedema but didn't disappoint. Mariona had the joint second most goals and assists of any WSL player — all while being a machine in midfield!

2

CAROLINE GRAHAM HANSEN

CLUB: Barcelona
POSITION: Winger
COUNTRY: Norway 🇳🇴
AGE: 30

CGH IS one of the wickedest wingers in the world! You can't take your eyes off the Norwegian's quick feet and slick dribbling style. She sends defenders spinning with her ace one-on-one ability and she's won league titles in THREE different countries — she's different gravy!

1

AITANA BONMATI

CLUB: Barcelona
POSITION: Midfielder
COUNTRY: Spain 🇪🇸
AGE: 27

THERE COULD only ever be one person at No.1, and that's Barca's Ballon d'Or baller, Aitana Bonmati. The Spanish superstar may not be the tallest or the fastest, but she makes up for that with tek that's off the charts. Her positioning, passing and footy IQ is from another planet!

ANSWERS!

Let's see if you smashed our QUIZZES. Get stuck into the answers so you can count your scores!

MASCOT MISMATCH!
PAGE 9

1 B, 2 B, 3 A, 4 B, 5 A, 6 A

A YEAR IN FOOTBALL!
PAGE 18

1 A, 2 B, 3 C, 4 B, 5 A, 6 B, 7 C, 8 A, 9 B

THE BIG PREM PHOTO-WORD!
PAGE 44

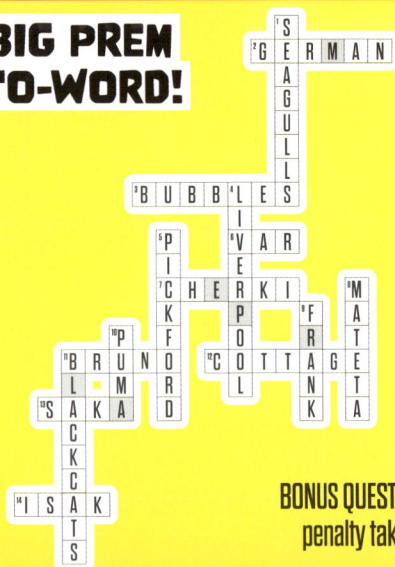

Crossword answers: SEAGULLS, GERMAN, BUBBLES, LIVERPOOL, VAR, PICKFORD, CHERKI, FRANK, MATETA, PALMER, BRUNO, BLACK CATS, ISAK

BONUS QUESTION: The Prem penalty taker is **Palmer**.

REAL OR WAX?
PAGES 46-47

Mary Earps A = real; B = wax,
Kylian Mbappe A = real; B = wax,
Cristiano Ronaldo A = real; B = wax,
Lionel Messi A = wax; B = real,
Manuel Neuer A = wax; B = real

WSL REWIND!
PAGE 61

1 Fran Kirby
2 Katie McCabe
3 Alex Greenwood
4 Vivianne Miedema
5 Hannah Hampton
6 Beth Mead
7 Bethany England
8 Rachel Daly
9 Khadija Shaw

KIDS QUIZ
PAGES 74-77

1 C, 2 B, 3 D, 4 C, 5 B, 6 C, 7 D, 8 D, 9 B, 10 D

ADULTS QUIZ

1 B, 2 B, 3 A, 4 B, 5 A, 6 B, 7 D, 8 D, 9 A, 10 A

Match of the Day Magazine

Telephone 020 7150 5136
Email inbox@motdmag.com

Editor — Mark Parry
Deputy Editor — Jake Wilson
Art Editors — Bradley Wooldridge, John Leonard
Features Editor — Sarah Johnson
Production Editor — Will Demetriou
Writer — Ollie Spencer

Managing Director — Alex Coates-Newman
Publisher — Igrain Roberts
Group Editor — Richard Clare
Freelance Designers — Pete Rogers, Alastair Pa
Iain Fryer
Annual images — Getty Images

BBC Books is an imprint of Ebury Publishing, One Embassy Gardens, 8 Viaduct Gardens, London SW11 7BW.
BBC Books is part of the Penguin Random House group of companies whose addresses can be found at global.
penguinrandomhouse.com. Copyright © BBC Match of the Day Magazine 2025. First published by BBC Books in 2025.
www.penguinrandomhouse.co.uk. A CIP catalogue record for this book is available from the British Library.
ISBN 9781785948398. Commissioning Editor: Albert DePetrillo Project Editor: Clementine Lussiana Production: Phil
Spencer. Printed and bound in Italy by Elcograf S.p.A. The authorised representative in the EEA is Penguin Random House
Ireland, Morrison Chambers, 32 Nassau Street, Dublin 2. Penguin Random House is committed to a sustainable future for
our business our readers and our planet. This book is made from Forest Stewardship Council ® certified paper.

BBC Match Of The Day Magazine is published by Immediate Media Company
London Limited under licence from BBC Studios Distribution Limited.
© Immediate Media Company London Limited 2025.

KHADIJA
SHAW

GOAL QUEEN!

JAMAICA

44 CAPS   57 GOALS

2026 FOOTY BINGO!

BINGO BINGO
15 22 35 52
15 3 17 41 60 66
7 30 59 75
9 28 48 67
1 21 44 50 71

Maybe these things will happen, maybe they wont... TICK 'EM if you see 'em!

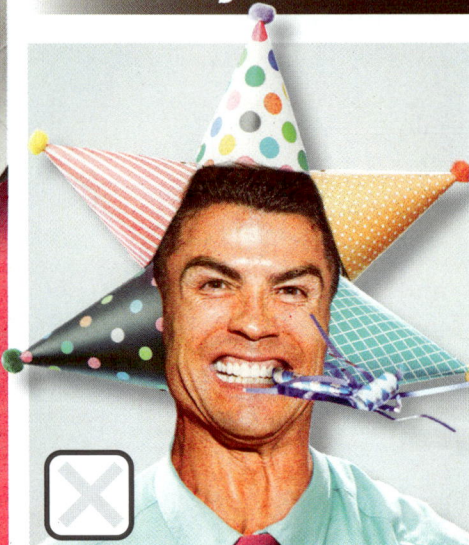

Cristiano Ronaldo invites you to his 41st birthday party!

This random wins the **Prem Golden Boot!**

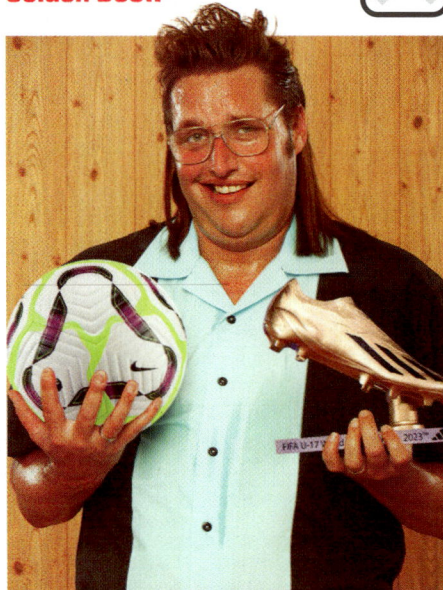

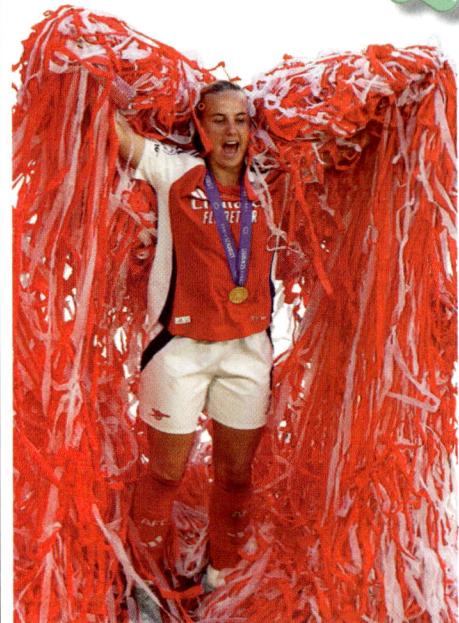

Beth Mead becomes a wrestler called Ribbon Girl!

Ella Toone becomes a Pokémon trainer!

Everton's new mascot is a sausage dog dressed as Superman!

Real Madrid sign ex-Man. United man **Jonny Evans**... for £90m!